AWDRY'S
STEAM RAILWAYS

To CHRISTINE
and Bookmark (Spalding)
with thanks.

AWDRY'S
STEAM RAILWAYS

CHRISTOPHER AWDRY

BOXTREE

Introduction

The one thing this book was not an attempt to do, was to find the best 'preserved' railway in Britain. My judgements, such as they were, would only have been subjective in any case. I have, it is true, expressed an opinion now and then. It would have been un-natural of me not to, and I would like to stress that such comments are no more than an opinion, and should not in any way be regarded as derogatory to the railway or management concerned.

In fact the summer was much better for not having to make decisions of this sort. I have been met with friendliness, courtesy and welcome by every railway I have visited, and collecting the material for this book has been a joy. My thanks to everyone I have encountered this year is boundless, and I am most grateful to all who have helped to smooth my path.

Apart from welcome, the other quality which came across, from everyone I met, was dedication. It has long been well known that without this our preserved railways would have succumbed ages ago. On the evidence of this year I can say, I believe without fear of contradiction, that dedication is alive and well all over the country. Long may it remain so.

Chris Awdry
Oundle, February 1995

Right *GWR-design Manor class 4-6-0 No.7828* Odney Manor *crosses the river Irwell at Burrs (East Lancashire Railway) against the sunset, with the 1600 Bury to Rawtenstall train on 31st January 1993.*

The Last Main Line
GREAT CENTRAL RAILWAY
Loughborough - Leicester

Coloured lights twinkled above the platform and on the canopy-high Christmas tree. Bunting fluttered, lit softly by the glow, and carols drifted from the PA system - in fact it was all very seasonal, apart from the weather, which was cold and damp. This was a Santa Special day, a week before Christmas on the Great Central Railway, and Loughborough station awaited an influx of excited youngsters for the 2pm train.

At 1.20 the one o'clock dining train for Leicester - points failures are not confined to British Rail - left noisily with much discharge of steam, and peace descended. Gradually the decibel count rose again, to climax at about ten minutes to two, when the carriages for the Santa train arrived. The currently-playing carol faded from the PA system.

"Will passengers for the two o'clock Santa Special train please see a uniformed member of staff, who will show them to their seats," it announced above the hubbub.

Santa Claus appeared, ringing a handbell, to the accompaniment of shrieks and laughter. Society volunteers emerged from one of the station offices and, laden with large boxes, staggered along the platform towards the front of the train. They loaded the boxes into a van while the locomotive, LNER Class A4 Pacific, *Sir Nigel Gresley*, named after its designer and resplendent in garter blue, joined the business end. A magnificent sight, and I smiled as I recalled being told, earlier in the day, of a letter from a passenger of the previous weekend, who had complained bitterly that her train had been pulled "...by a blue diesel." Sir Nigel must have been almost giddy in his grave!

This, of course, was the view as the passengers saw it. What they did not see, and what many of them probably took for granted, was the work that had to be done before the train could leave the platform. The timetabling, done in all likelihood a year in advance, the care taken to ensure that no-one is disappointed because two people need to

Left *Austerity 0-6-0ST No.7597 approaches Quorn & Woodhouse station heading a southbound passenger train in January 1989.*

Great Central Railway

Loughborough Central Station, Great Central
Road, Loughborough, Leics, LE11 1RW.
Tel. 01509 230726

Route	Loughborough - Leicester North (8 miles)
Gauge	Standard
Open	W/e, b/h throughout the year; midweek trains some Tuesdays.

In 1889 the Manchester, Sheffield & Lincolnshire
Railway promised the Great Northern Railway
that it would not seek to build railways south of a
place called Annesley, near Nottingham. Ten years
later, under the thin disguise of a new name, the
Great Central Railway opened a line southwards
to London. It was a line built for fast traffic, with
not a single level crossing in its length, but it failed
to fulfil the hopes of its promoters. Last in the field,
it was the first main line to go, in 1969. The section
between Loughborough and Quorn was revived
by a preservation society in 1973: since then
expansion (to Rothley in 1975, Leicester North in
1991) has been steady, and plans are in hand for a
stretch of double track and even a length of
quadruple track - just like the big railway! Big
engines too, many of them visitors, can be seen
and enjoyed here, and a very fruitful link has been
established with the Birmingham Railway
Museum at Tyseley, which provides much of this
interchange of stock.

Above *Ex-GCR Director class 4-4-0* Butler-
Henderson *at Loughborough on 21st February
1992, carrying its BR number 62660.*

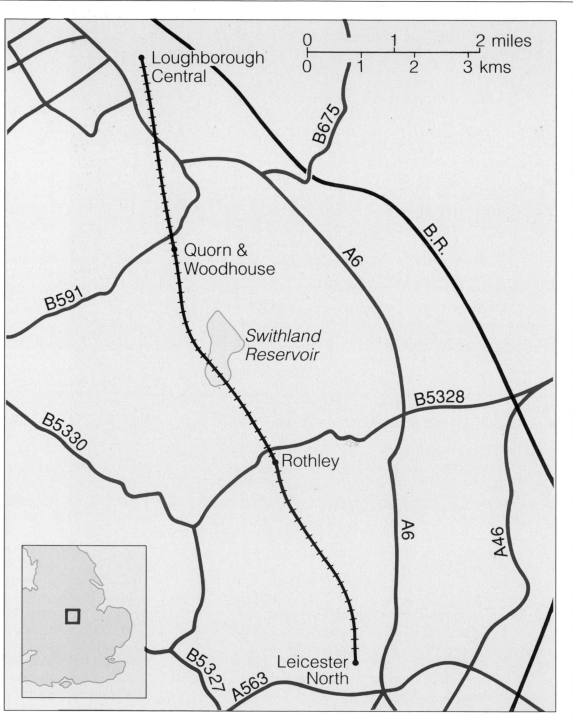

compete for the same seat, the organising of the presents, and the arranging (well in advance, for Santa is a busy person) of the essential man's visit. Station and carriages need decorating, buffet supplies must be ordered, and the locomotives have to be rostered, not to mention the drivers and firemen to work them. Bear in mind too that most of this work is done by volunteers. Someone had had to be at the locomotive shed at 6.30 that morning to light the fires in the engines. The drivers had to be there early to oil them and make sure all was well. Others had been there to clean them.

The Great Central Railway has ten full-time employees. The rest of the work is done by a dedicated band of volunteers, each doing a job they choose to do, though there must of necessity be a good deal of flexibility. Nigel Lawrey, who showed me round the shed early that morning, is a volunteer. He comes from Leicester, visits Loughborough about every other week, and is obviously very happy there.

"After a bit," he told me, "you get to know what jobs need doing, and if you can see that no one else is doing them on a particular day, you muck in and do it yourself."

He has had firing turns on the engines, and will, in time no doubt, graduate to driving them. But an aspiring driver needs patience.

"Quite a number of volunteers turn up full of enthusiasm," he said as we went in search of oil and paraffin with which to clean the motion of *Sir Nigel Gresley*. "They get disappointed because they don't get to drive an engine first time out, and we don't see 'em again."

"Over the months," he went on, "you get to know the blokes who come at the same time as you do, and you begin to work together. Not an official team, but it helps if you've got a mate; it's someone to talk to, and some jobs can't be done singlehanded anyway."

By this time the morning light had strengthened enough for us to see what we were doing as we made a start at cleaning the motion and wheels of the alleged 'blue diesel'. At the same time the engine crew was underneath, raking out the grate and checking the inside motion.

"Most of us have two sets of overalls," said Nigel, "the drivers in particular." He pointed between the wheels. "That job he does in one set, but you'll never see him driving in dirty ones."

At about 9.30 the big blue engine moved off shed and

Nigel and I turned our attention to the other engine for the day, No 35005 *Canadian Pacific*, or 'CP' for short. This is a 4-6-2 designed by Oliver Bulleid for the Southern Railway, and built in 1941, one of a class named after merchant shipping companies. A revolutionary design in its day, the engine was rebuilt by British Railways and after withdrawal languished for some time at Carnforth in Lancashire. Privately purchased, it arrived in Loughborough in 1989, and was returned to steam here in 1991. The engine's driver for the day was to be Geoff White, from the Birmingham Railway Museum at Tyseley, an ex-BR steam driver.

The 1993/4 edition of *Railways Restored* lists 20 steam engines based at Loughborough. Not all are owned by the railway, however, and in addition the line sees many visiting engines. This situation has become much more fluid of late, following an exchange agreement with

Above LNER Peppercorn design class A2 4-6-2 No.60532 Blue Peter hurries south of Woodthorpe at the head of a rake of 'blood & custard' stock in October 1992.

Right Ex-SR Schools class 4-4-0 No.30926 Repton *stands outside Loughborough shed on 29th January 1993.*

Right Ex-SR Schools class 4-4-0 No.30926 Repton *stands outside Loughborough shed on 29th January 1993.*

Left 'Big blue diesel' jibes notwithstanding, ex LNER A4 class 4-6-2 No.4498 Sir Nigel Gresley *makes a fine sight at Thurcaston, southbound in January 1994.*

Birmingham Railway Museum which has already resulted in several 'Tyseley' engines spending time on the GC.

Another resident which may be on show is Class Y7 No.68088, a tiny 0-4-0 tank engine of North Eastern Railway origin, built at Darlington in 1921. Rather larger is ex-GWR No.6990 *Witherslack Hall*, a 4-6-0 of the 'Modified Hall' Class. This engine was a regular on the Paddington to Worcester service for many years, and turned in some notable high-speed runs. It was withdrawn from Bristol in 1966, but had to wait nine years before arriving at Loughborough in the November of 1975. Restoration took even longer, and it was eleven more years before, on 6th September 1986, it finally re-entered traffic.

Only two examples of LNER Class B1 4-6-0 remain in captivity, as it were, and both are connected with the GCR. For many years No.1306 *Mayflower* was here, but is now away undergoing overhaul. The other is No.1264, built in 1947 by the North British Loco Company, and owned by the Thompson B1 Locomotive Society who rescued the engine from Barry scrapyard during 1975. It was then discovered that the boiler was impossible to repair, but undaunted the Society set to work. Now, two decades later, the job is almost done.

One of the commonest types of locomotive in preservation is the Stanier Class 5MT (mixed traffic to you and me) 4-6-0 of the LMS, and the GCR has its example, No.5231, owned by Michael Stephenson. This engine was built by Armstrong Whitworth's of Newcastle in 1936, and withdrawn from Carnforth in 1968. It was at once acquired by its present owner, who moved it to Loughborough in 1973 - apart from a while out of service during a major overhaul, and a spell on the Nene Valley Railway, the engine has worked here ever since.

Undergoing overhaul during my recent visit was

No.69523, a Class N2 0-6-2 tank engine built for the Great Northern Railway in 1921 by the North British Locomotive Company, to the design of Sir Nigel Gresley. These engines were used for the suburban services out of Kings Cross, and this example is fitted with the condensing pipes necessary to allow it to work through the Underground to Moorgate. It was a Kings Cross engine for 40 years, and was finally withdrawn at Peterborough in September 1962. The engine was preserved by the Gresley Society using its LNER number, 4744, and worked for some years on the Keighley & Worth Valley Railway, appearing in the feature film *The Railway Children* in 1975. It was then moved to Loughborough, and returned to service in 1978. The regulator on this engine is placed high up, and the story is told of the very short driver who used to reach it by standing on a box. Until, that is, the day when someone used the box to light the fire...

The biggest engine at Loughborough is BR Standard Class 9F 2-10-0 No.92212. These engines were introduced in 1954, and many, including this one, saw service on the GC line, so to have one of the class here is appropriate. The engine reached Loughborough in the autumn of 1979,

Right *Ex-LMS Jubilee class 4-6-0 No.5593* Kolhapur *leaves Rothley for Leicester North on the 1000 train, 11th January 1992.*

Below *Ex-LMS Stanier Class 5MT 4-6-0 No.45231 passes Woodthorpe with a 'windcutter' train on 4th June 1993.*

and restoration is continuing. While on the subject of BR Standards, it should be mentioned that most of the restoration work on Standard Pacific No.71000 *Duke of Gloucester* took place at Loughborough.

No.34039 *Boscastle* was the first locomotive to arrive at Loughborough, in 1973. Built in 1946 at Brighton, it is one of 110 'West Country' Class Pacifics designed by Bulleid for the Southern Railway, and was rebuilt to its present form in 1959. After withdrawal in 1965 it spent seven years at Barry, from where it was rescued by James Tawse - the engine returned to service in 1994.

Boscastle is a lighter version of Bulleid's design for the Merchant Navy Class and, therefore, of *Canadian Pacific*, which was the main concern of Nigel and myself at present. Because there was shunting to do, our time was limited, and there was no opportunity for more than a fairly swift rub over the motion on both sides. The wheels had to look after themselves. When that engine too had gone away towards the station, both ashpits needed cleaning out - not just of ash either, but of smokebox sludge (a distinctly obnoxious mixture of ash and oil) too - and hosing down. This was a wheelbarrow and shovel job, and, in the pit nearest the shed, a wet-foot job too, since the fall from the drain is very shallow, and water has sometimes to be persuaded to leave. After that, Nigel and I went to the messroom for a well-earned cup of tea.

Not everyone jumped for joy when the Manchester, Sheffield & Lincolnshire Railway announced that it proposed to extend its line southwards from Annesley (north of Nottingham) to London. The Great Northern Railway must have been particularly peeved, since the MS&L had made an undertaking to it in 1889 that it would not come south of Annesley. The Midland Railway too must have been less than happy, since for the 25-odd miles between Nottingham and Leicester the new line more or less paralleled its own.

Notwithstanding Parliamentary objections, the last of the major main lines was opened to carry passengers to a new terminus at Marylebone on 15th March 1899, though the line had been used for coal since the previous year. Manchester, Sheffield & Lincolnshire had sounded a somewhat provincial title, at odds with the company's aspirations, and so it was changed to the Great Central

Left No.5593 Kolhapur *again heading south, this time in brighter weather on the same day, 11th January 1992.*

Railway just before services began. In fact the aspirations, may have been those of the company Chairman, Sir Edward Watkin. He dreamed of a through route to the Continent via the South Eastern Railway (of which he was also Chairman) and a tunnel, so construction was made to the loading gauge, used in Europe, slightly larger than the British standard. The line was laid out for speed - gradients were easy and there were no level crossings in the entire length of the London extension, but because other railways had reached both Nottingham and Leicester first, those cities had to be crossed on viaducts,

and Victoria station in Nottingham lay in a deep cutting with a tunnel at either end.

It was thus an expensive line to build, and the amount of traffic it generated was disappointing. The argument rages to this day as to whether the cost was justified, but whatever one's view, the GCR became a part of the London & North Eastern Railway at the Grouping in 1923. As time went on the fast trains were transferred to other routes, and the Great Central route became something of a poor relation. The LNER was not a wealthy concern anyway, and perhaps saw the route as something of a

Above Swithland Reservoir is a favourite haunt of photographers. It was a clear day there on 9th November 1991 as ex-SR Schools class No.30926 Repton hurried south with the 1145 Loughborough-Leicester North train.

millstone around its neck. After World War 2 British Railways attempted to do something with the line, and fast services returned, but one suspects the nationalised company met the same problems as the LNER had. The London to Manchester service was withdrawn in 1960, and by September six years later all services north of Nottingham had gone. In 1969 BR decided to retain the Midland route, and from 5th May that year the GC line was abandoned.

Some of those who saw closure writing on the wall saw also the possibilities for a preservation scheme. Just before the line closed, the Main Line Preservation Group was formed, with a view to "...acquiring a suitable length of main line for the operation of steam-hauled passenger trains at realistic speeds."

The entire 23.5-mile stretch between Nottingham and Leicester was hoped for at first, but this soon proved too costly and unmanageable a project. By 1971 the group had scaled down its objectives and re-named itself the Main Line Steam Trust. Priority was to be given to a link with BR at Loughborough or the reinstatement of a quarry line diverging at Swithland Junction. The Trust at this stage had two main line engines, *King Haakon VII*, a 2-6-0 built in Sweden in 1919, and named after the monarch it had carried to safety from the German invasion in 1940, and Southern Railway No.34039 *Boscastle*. The latter, as we have seen, is now back in service after a long-term restoration, but *King Haakon VII* moved to the Bressingham Steam Museum in 1982.

Though it needed much attention, Loughborough Central station was intact, and it was leased, with part of the yard. Track, however, was another matter. To begin with this also was 'leased', under an agreement that BR would leave it in place in exchange for a payment of £1,000 per month. On 30th September 1973 Jimmy Bloomfield, manager of the Leicester City Football Club opened the section between Loughborough and Quorn. A train hauled by No.5231 left at midday, the first official train - trains had run earlier, but these had been private, members-only jobs. No.5231 left Quorn at 12.30, and passed a second train, hauled by *Robert Nelson* No.4, the first time trains in motion had passed each other between stations on a preserved line. This engine had been the first to be steamed on the GCR, and now works on the Gloucestershire Warwickshire Railway.

The opening to Rothley (almost 5 miles from

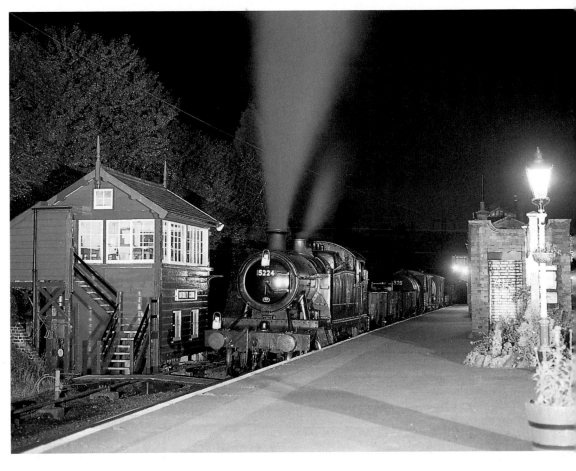

Loughborough) took place on 6th September 1975, but soon afterwards came an ultimatum from BR Properties Board. Unless the line was purchased by 1st April 1976, it announced, the track would be lifted. This placed the MLST in a quandary, for, since it was a charitable trust, funds with which to buy the track could not be raised by a share issue. A new company, Great Central Railway (1976) Ltd was formed, and the share issue opened in May 1976, with a deadline for line purchase of 1st July that year. The minimum amount required was set at £135,000, and this was just - only just - achieved, so that 2.75 miles of track could be bought. BR agreed to an extension of time until the end of the year, to give the Company a chance to raise enough to buy as far as Rothley, but it lifted the remaining single track southwards to Birstall from there. Yet another extension was granted to 20th January 1977, and on the 19th a cheque

Above *Night freight on the Great Central Railway. Ex-GWR 5205 class 2-8-0T No.5224 stands at Rothley on 1st October 1992.*

Far left *Ex-London Transport's GWR-design 0-6-0PT No.L90 (visiting from the Buckinghamshire Railway Centre) heads north from Rothley with a mixed freight in July 1993.*

was handed over for £250,000. This however had been achieved only by means of a bankloan and several interest-free loans from members. Charnwood Borough council bought the remaining 100 acres of land required for the subsequent extension to Birstall, and leased it to the railway.

Five weeks' work to 9th October 1976 saw a new loop and ground-frame laid in just south of Loughborough station, and development since has been steady. Our train heads past these installations - between the station bridge and the next, on the left of the line (facing forwards) are the premises of Ladybird Books. After this bridge come two more, the first being a crossing by the A6 trunk road.

Woodthorpe cutting, a spot beloved of photographers, comes beyond the bridges, and the line emerges on an embankment to reveal rolling arable countryside. Not spectacular when measured, say against the Vale of Rheidol or West Highland lines, but one hardly expects that in rural Leicestershire. Soon the train plunges into cutting again, under a bridge, and draws to a halt in Quorn & Woodhouse station. This has an island platform with the access at the north end, from the bridge we have just come under. On the left is the railway's access for road-borne stock arrivals, and an open space which was once the goods yard. Now it is a car-park.

A long embankment follows, and signs of quarrying activity around Mountsorrel can be seen away to the left. Opposite is a wooded ridge and Beacon Hill, with, to the south, another summit topped by a folly called Old John Tower. Between is an area of nature trails and country parks. Soon the line dives into cutting again, to surface on Swithland viaduct.

Right Ex-SR Merchant Navy class 4-6-2 No.35005 Canadian Pacific *blasts a way past Woodthorpe with a southbound train from Loughborough on 23rd November 1991.*

Left Ex-GNR Stirling 'Single' No.1 spent a short while on loan to the GCR from the National Railway Museum during 1982. Here the engine steams towards Rothley, then the southern terminus of the line, in May.

loops are short, and used for the storage of stock when not in use for demonstration purposes.

One of the items they 'house' is the rake of 20 steel open coal wagons, bought after an appeal by the monthly magazine *Steam Railway*, and used for the first time on 7th November 1992, when contributors to the appeal were treated to a passenger ride behind LNER Class A2 4-6-2 *Blue Peter*. The train halted here for a runpast by No.5224 with its 'windcutters'. This ex-GWR 2-8-0 tank engine, built in 1924, had been withdrawn by BR in 1963, having worked in South Wales on just this sort of train for most of its life. It reached Loughborough in 1978, where it steamed again in October 1984, the first ex-Barry scrapyard engine to be restored on the Great Central. Working parties are now being organised at Swithland to preserve the wagons for the future, and it must be hoped that after the initial euphoria of achievement the set is not simply allowed to rust away as it becomes a drain on resources.

The problem with freight vehicles on preserved lines, of course, is that they do not, unlike carriages, generate any income. Certain railways, to their great credit, are making a feature of freight trains these days, some trains being chartered by photographers for their own professional purposes. An exception, so far as photographic commission is concerned, is the East Lancashire Railway, which in 1994 ran a short goods train from Bury up to Ramsbottom before the start of each day's passenger timetable, and brought it back again when it had finished. Such operations add interest to the railway fare and also create a use for stock, some of it beautifully restored, which otherwise is totally unremunerative. And unless it is used in this way, there is little point in restoring it, since no-one but the restorers (and perhaps a few die-hard enthusiasts) would ever see it! Wagons have been the cinderellas of the preservation movement for far too long; the fact that they don't show a 'money' return is really no reason to hide them away.

The train's next stop is Rothley, a station very similar in layout to Quorn, even down to the ex-goods yard on the east side. Again, this is now a car-park, and a modern shed has been erected at the south end, with approach lines facing south. Unlike Quorn however, Rothley is a passing loop, and a signalbox, resited from Blind Lane, Wembley, went into service here in March 1992.

South of Rothley the line crosses Rothley Brook. The

Above Ex-GWR 5205 class 2-8-0T No.5224 heads a mixed freight just south of Woodthorpe on 1st October 1992.

Far right On loan from the Birmingham Railway Museum at Tyseley, ex-GWR Castle class 4-6-0 No. 7029 Clun Castle crosses Swithland viaduct on 26th December 1993.

This is actually two viaducts, linked by a short length of embankment on an island in the centre of the reservoir, but the whole structure is about half a mile long.

About this point one suddenly realises that the train is on double track. Not effective double track at present, admittedly, for there are bufferstops at each end of the section, and a crossover only at the southern end, but it looks good. On the left the formation opens out and a newly-built shed comes into view, with a whole array of sidings south of it, welcome storage space for a large collection of stock. A branch to the Mountsorrel workings once left the main line here, and for a short stretch the railway is actually four-track, again creating an impression of main line running. This is the result of a donation of £300,000 spread over 4 yearly instalments, under which doubling of track is projected for the entire distance from Loughborough to Rothley. At present the

village of Thurcaston, away to the west, is actually closer to the railway than the community from which the station takes its name, but the old GCR, in the manner of many others, simply named its station after what it perceived as the more important of the two places. The embankment here is higher than it appears, for the slopes are well wooded and the growth cuts off the view to the foot of the banks.

A bridleway crosses the line by an overbridge, and the embankment resumes once more, from which further signs of habitation can be seen to the east. This is the outskirts of Leicester, but cutting screens most of the houses from the railway. Finally, with a whistle, the train steams below a substantial overbridge and draws to a halt in what is currently the only platform at Leicester North station.

Leicester North is built to the south of the site of the old Belgrave & Birstall station - if you look back towards the bridge you will see above the central pier the bricked-up entrance to the platforms. It was of the same pattern as the two we have recently passed. The present station, for which there are ambitious - and expensive - plans, was opened officially on 5th July 1991 as part of the celebrations to commemorate the 150th anniversary to Thomas Cook's first railway excursion. That too ran from Loughborough to Leicester, but along the Midland line not this one - this line was still almost 60 years in the future! Leicester North will be the southern terminus of the preserved GC line, and will, it is hoped, resemble the centre roads of the Great Central station at Marylebone, complete with canopy. The massive hydraulic buffers from the London station are already in place.

With this project in hand, and the northern extension also in the melting pot, the GCR has plenty to think about just at the moment. It is intended that a site at Ruddington - just south of Nottingham - should be developed as a Heritage Centre, with the ultimate aim of extending the railway southwards towards Loughborough. A new company has been formed to build this section, but though it will fulfil the original aim of the Main Line Steam Trust, one hears the wisdom of the move questioned. There is a limit to the amount

Left No shortage of steam from ex-LNER A4 class 4-6-2 No.4498 Sir Nigel Gresley, *Thurcaston, 16th January 1994.*

a visitor can pay in fares, particularly if the family is of any size, and the fare for the whole trip will necessarily be higher than it is for the present distance. It should not be taken for granted therefore that passengers are, willy-nilly, going to travel the whole length of the line. Several of the longer lines are already facing this problem, and the way that they address it will no doubt influence the GCR's future actions.

A first steam engine has gone to Ruddington, and the prospect of grant aid for the extension is being examined. The disused section from Ruddington to Rushcliffe Halt was valued by BR at £87,500 - the Railway has to find £32,000, and Nottinghamshire County Council and Rushcliffe Borough Council have agreed to fund the rest. The need for volunteers will become even more vital, not only to man the trains, but also to carry out the work that the public rarely sees - the engine cleaners, the ashpit clearers, the fitters, the man who drives the JCB that puts the coal in the tender. And of course, those unsung heroes who do the muckiest job of all, the engine disposal crews. Small wonder, it has to be said, that the 'I just want to drive' brigade go away disillusioned.

Driving a steam engine is a job that has to be learned by experience, through the stages (or grades, as they are called) of cleaning, firing and maintenance. Only when, over a period of time, that experience has been acquired can one possibly understand sufficient about the way the machine works to drive it safely. Would you, as a passenger, knowingly want to entrust yourself to a train powered by someone standing on the footplate for the first time? Without stalwarts like Nigel Lawrey and his mates, people who are prepared to learn and do the job safely and properly, the railway simply couldn't function.

"We advertise driving courses," Geoff Parton, the Traffic Manager told me, "but I sometimes think we ought to offer disposal courses too."

Perhaps some would pay for the privilege of getting filthy. Promoted perhaps as "Enjoy the dirty bits..." it might do quite well. There's a thought to conjure with!

Right *A short mixed freight approaches Leicester North on 1st May 1992 behind ex-LNER Y7 class 0-4-0T No.68088.*

Island Line
ISLE OF WIGHT STEAM RAILWAY
Smallbrook Junction - Wootton

All the railways built on the Isle of Wight failed, in some degree, to make as much money as their promoters had hoped, some a good deal more disastrously than others. There was a good deal of opposition to their coming anyway - many Islanders argued that improved transport facilities would encourage people to go to Portsmouth or Southampton, quite forgetting than there might equally be a traffic flow from the other direction. The first line to get past the resistance eventually obtained Parliamentary approval in 1859: it was to run between Cowes and Newport, and opened three years later.

The new railway was unable to realise its full potential until a link between Ryde and Newport had been put in - this was the Ryde & Newport Railway, and the Act of Parliament authorising it gained Royal Assent on 25th July 1872. The line ran north-east from Newport to Wootton, where it turned south-eastwards through Havenstreet - the station was renamed Haven Street on 9th June 1958 - before curving north-east again at Ashey to (later) Smallbrook Junction. From here it travelled north for a mile and a half to a terminus at Ryde. It is the five-mile section between Wootton and Smallbrook Junction which survives today as the Isle of Wight Steam Railway.

The Company was granted capital of £60,000 for its eight miles of line, and given borrowing powers up to £21,600. The line's engineers were George Young and H. D. Martin: the contractors until 1874 were Barnett & Gale, whose place until completion was then taken by James Taylor of Poole. The railway opened on 20th December 1875, but Martin, who had been working traffic on the line between Cowes and Newport, declined to do the same with the longer route, refusing to let his engines to run beyond Newport "...without extra charge". So the Company decided to operate the trains for itself, and promptly hired Martin's engines with which to do it!

Left Ex-IWCR 0-6-0T No.11 drops down towards Haven Street in August 1989. Carriage No.46 (see text) is next to the engine.

Isle of Wight Steam Railway

Haven Street Station, Ryde,
Isle of Wight, PO33 4DS.
Tel. 01983 882204

Route   Smallbrook Junction - Wootton
              (5 miles)
Gauge   Standard
Open   Varies according to time of year -
              please telephone for details.

The Ryde & Newport Railway was only the second line on the Island, and was not authorised until 1872. It opened for business in 1875. The mainland railway companies took an interest, and the line survived on a sequence of hand-me-down stock, which contributes greatly to the atmosphere of the preserved line today. BR closed the system finally in 1966 (except for the Ryde to Shanklin section) and moves towards preservation began at once. Now the mood of a country branch line is wonderfully evoked at Haven Street - small engines ply gently along a short but quite hilly line, with scarcely a car in sight. Passengers travel in beautifully restored timber carriages, many with an interesting history and most having a connection with the Island and its railways. Connection can be made with the electrified Island Line at Smallbrook Junction, for travel on to Ryde or the resorts on the east coast of the Island.

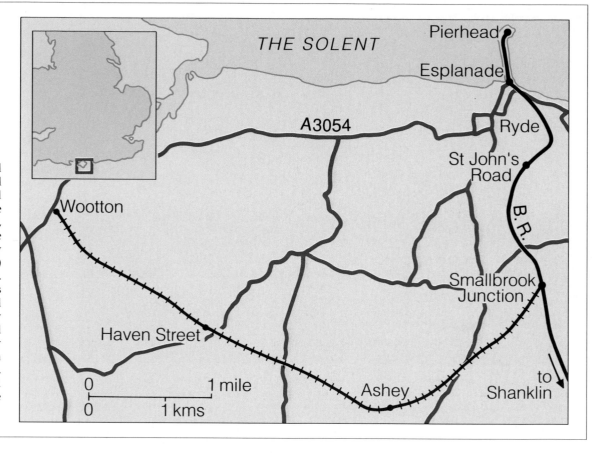

Far right Ex-LSWR O2 class 0-4-4T No.24 Calbourne *tops the summit of the line near Ashey with a Smallbrook Junction to Haven Street train on 3rd September 1991.*

Suffice at this point perhaps, to say that both the London & South Western and the London, Brighton & South Coast Railways had interests in the Island lines, and kept them supplied with second (or even third) -hand stock. Since this was often a good way beyond its youth, the men became adept at making do, and it is really due only to them that the preservationists on the Island have anything to preserve. By the time the Southern Railway came upon the scene at the 1923 Grouping, only four out of the original nine independent railway companies on the Island had survived to be taken over. BR appeared in due course, but despite a passenger upsurge during the years immediately after the War, traffic soon began to drift to the roads. By the early 1950s only the Ryde to Ventnor route, serving as it did the resorts on the east coast of the Island, remained viable.

From 1952 closures began. By 1964 only the Ventnor line and the Ryde-Newport route remained, and even these were threatened, for not only had the Beeching Report recommended complete closure of the Island lines, but also a Committee, set up by Ryde Council in 1963, had deliberated whether the remaining lines should be closed willy-nilly and converted to roads. Though these mandarins had to concede that the resulting roads would be totally inadequate to cope with the summer influx of visitors to Sandown and Shanklin, total closure of the lines was nevertheless advertised in 1964. Legal objections prevented it, and a failure to organise local bus services kept them open through 1965.

The Ryde to Cowes line closed on 21st February 1966, and the Shanklin to Ventnor section two months later. Steam remained on what was left until 31st December, when the service was temporarily withdrawn for the railway to be converted to electric traction. It re-opened

on 20th March 1967 with a service run by ex-London Transport underground trains, an arrangement which remains today. The other line, between Wootton and Smallbrook Junction, has managed to retain an atmosphere much more like that of 1966 - an 'old-time branch line' as the current marketing puts it.

During 1966 a Company called Vectrail was formed to consider re-opening the entire route between Cowes and Ryde. The Wight Locomotive Society was also formed to establish a museum for the Island's historic railway relics. It had a base at Newport station, where BR allowed members access to renovate stock already collected, an activity which was, reported *Railway World* in March 1968, "... proceeding apace". Three coaches were earmarked for preservation, and another of the Society's objectives was to obtain an Adams 0-4-4 tank engine, No.24 *Calbourne*, which was then in store at Ryde. By the end of 1968 £1,000 had been collected towards this end, and a further £500 was still required. *Calbourne* finally reached Newport in August 1969, having cost a pittance by today's standards, but a sum that was then a great deal to the young Society.

Calbourne was built in the London & South Western Works at Nine Elms, Battersea in 1891 as No.209, to a design of William Adams. Adams had a talent for producing shapely engines - the 4-4-2 tank No.488 on the Bluebell Railway is perhaps the most notable - and his O2 class of 0-4-4 tank engines was no exception. The Isle of Wight Central Railway, needing a locomotive, inspected No.209 in 1908, but seems not to have been impressed. It was only after the Southern Railway decided that the O2 class would be ideal motive power for the Island lines that No.209 came across the Solent, landing at Medina Wharf, Cowes in April 1925.

It was renumbered W24, and, in September 1928, named *Calbourne*. The engine had been destined for work on the Ventnor West branch, but it soon became clear that W24 was much too good and powerful for such mundane duties. It was allocated to Ryde shed in 1930, and during the 1940s was regularly at work on the Ryde-Newport line. W24 remained in service to the end, and, with W31 *Chale*, was retained by BR until March 1967 to work engineers' and track-lifting trains. It was then

Left The cab interior of ex-LB&SCR A1X class 0-6-0T No.W8 Freshwater, at Haven Street on 27th September 1994.

scheduled for breaking up, had not the Wight Locomotive Society come to the rescue.

In 1970 Vectrail abandoned its scheme, and the WLS at once moved in. Protracted negotiations with BR had resulted in the saving of Haven Street station from demolition, and the Isle of Wight County Council had bought the trackbed. At the beginning of 1971 the Society was given just five days notice to leave Newport station, which was scheduled for demolition. Four special trains, hauled by *Calbourne*, hauled the stock to Haven Street on 24th January. Within days, contractors had moved in and severed the rail link with Newport.

The new headquarters was derelict and forlorn, having stood unused for five years. By May some progress had

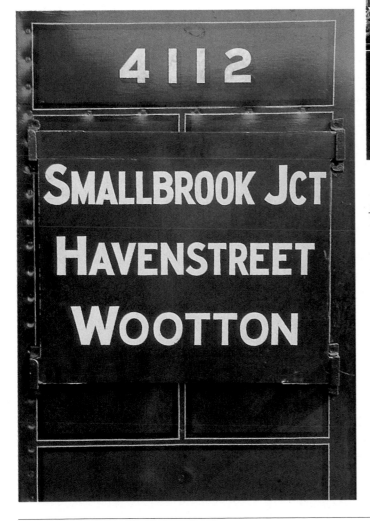

Above *The right-hand front cab spectacle of W8* Freshwater *gets a polish in the yard at Haven Street, 27th September 1994. The bunker on the right belongs to Austerity 0-6-0ST No.198* Royal Engineer.

Left *The destination board on carriage No.4112, Haven Street, in September 1994.*

been made, and agreement reached with the County Council for the lease of former railway land between the Society's new base and Wootton. Steam days on alternate Sunday afternoons during 1971 drew 9,000 visitors, and in the meantime volunteers had begun to rebuild the line. The original station at Wootton had been closed in 1953, but this was not greatly significant since a landslip had, in any case, made the site inaccessible. A new terminus was planned, 100 yards short of the old station, and as this would require the removal of 22,000 cubic yards of infill from a cutting, a contractor was drafted in. An inaugural train used the new loop on 22nd August 1977, and no fewer than 45,359 passengers were carried during the year. Wootton was merely a run-round point at this time - it was to be another ten years before a proper station was opened.

Work was continuing at Haven Street too. By 1974 an engine inspection pit had been built, and a 'balloon' water-tank, rescued from Newport, had been raised. Planning permission was being sought to establish a workshop and

Above Austerity 0-6-0ST *No.198* Royal Engineer *leaves Ashey station en route for Haven Street on 27th September 1994.*

Far right Ex-IWCR 0-6-0T *No.11 (ex-LB&SCR A1X class) heads away from Haven Street towards Wootton during August 1989.*

locomotive storage shed: a single-road shed was envisaged, 89 feet long and incorporating a wheeldrop - the shed would have a lean-to alongside as further covered storage. Clearly the visitors who came liked what they saw. More than 50,000 of them (53,750 to be precise) came in 1978, and 59,167 tickets were sold in the following year. Work at Haven Street continued through the early 1980s, and the foundation stone for a museum block was laid on 18th August 1983 by Sir John Nicholson, Bt, KBE, CIE, the Lord Lieutenant of the Island, assisted by Mark Starling, one of the railways Manpower Services Commission trainees. The building would include materials rescued from the Totland Bay Hotel, and estimates put the cost of it at £40,000.

Passenger carryings fell after the 1979 peak, but by 1985 had recovered almost to the 50,000 mark. Trackbed clearance by the MSC party had been going on between Haven Street and Ashey, the next station towards Smallbrook Junction, and the new station at Wootton was expected to be open by 17 August 1986. In the event an opening ceremony was actually performed on 31st May

1987 by Chris Green, then Director of Network SouthEast. During his speech he took the opportunity to announce that redundant rail and sleepers arising from the planned singling of the Brading to Sandown section of the coastal line could be available to the steam railway very cheaply, if other sponsors could be encouraged to help. If a feasibility study showed that the scheme was viable, he thought that the railway "...should be thinking in terms of a two-year timescale".

The feasibility study indicated that the project *was* viable, and that it would cost around £600,000. A go-ahead was endorsed by a massive 98% of the membership, clearance work began in June and July 1989 and 3,400 sleepers and 424 rails were salvaged and moved to the Haven Street end of the extension. A first track-panel was laid by Chris Green on 25th August that year. The possibility of running alongside BR to Ryde St. John's Road had been rejected in 1988, and, as a result, the present Smallbrook Junction station was built in 1991. The Smallbrook link seems to have benefited both parties, for approximately 15 per cent of the steam line's business is estimated to be coming from that end.

"This Railway has problems which you might not meet with anywhere else," Terry Hastings, the Marketing and Traffic Manager explained. "It's largely due to our position, on an island, of course, but because volunteers are not easy to come by we need to employ 9 full-time and 9 part-time staff. We rely on them to run the railway at times when volunteers numbers are low. There is a core of about 200 volunteers, in total, about 50 of whom come regularly"

"It does get a bit tight at times," he agreed, answering the obvious question, "but we have to live with that. We are expanding our season too, which was once just the holiday months and a bit at Christmas. The summer season is now growing at each end, which, of course, puts more pressure on staff and volunteers, and there is a limit to what you can ask even a very dedicated volunteer to do. But we have a good spirit here, and a good atmosphere too, which seems to rub off on our visitors. This year, 1994, I shall be hoping to top the half-million mark in turnover."

One of the reasons why Haven Street retains its vintage railway atmosphere is the 'hand-me-downs' that the Island railways had always been stocked with. There are very few preserved lines which do not run the ubiquitous

Above Ready for the 'right away'. Class A1X No.8's departure from Haven Street for Wootton seems imminent, 27th September 1994.

the carriage took to the rails in public for the first time on 3rd August 1986. I can vouch from personal experience that the coach, now numbered 6336 and superbly finished in olive green, is a joy to ride in.

Three firms contributed to the restoration - Westinghouse donated a set of brake equipment, Pilkington Brothers plc supplied toughened glass for the windows, and Trucast Ltd of Ryde supplied replica grabrails and door-handles. The TVS Charitable Trust made a grant with which springing equipment was bought and the drawgear shortened. Thanks to their help and the hard work of the volunteers involved, the trophy for the 1986 ARPS award for the Best Restored Coach was presented to the railway on 20th September 1987, during a ceremony at Haven Street. That was an exceptionally proud moment, because at the same ceremony the railway also won the award for the Best Restored Station, and a plaque to mark this achievement was unveiled at the station.

Because Haven Street is in the middle of the line, a round trip involves a second, intermediate call at the station. Let us start our journey at Wootton, since this was one of the original termini. As we have seen, this was opened in 1986, and consists of a single platform to the south of the line, on which a luggage van body serves as shelter, and a run-round loop. The ticket office, which stands beyond the buffer-stops, was a shelter for porters and ticket collectors at Ryde Pier Head, and the ground-frame served first as a signalbox at Newport and Freshwater, and, until rescued by the railway, as a bus shelter. Both these buildings are smartly painted in a yellowish cream, with green frames.

Our engine will make a very smart run-round here, and as we leave we pass an engineer's siding to the north of the line. South of the line lies grazing land, sloping gently, but to the north the countryside is more wooded. The line begins to fall at 1 in 61 according to the books, though I was told by more than one member that the pull to the summit at Ashey is the steepest part of the line at 1 in 67! The line is falling almost continuously, and as we pass beneath an overbridge the workshop building at Haven Street becomes visible ahead, on the outside of a gentle curve.

The main building and the platform presently at Haven Street were built in 1926 - no doubt the newly-arrived SR found previous arrangements not to its liking. The building now used as the booking office served as a crossing keeper's hut at Cowes until 1966. The building nearby, bearing the date 1866, and now converted to use as a shop, museum, and staff messroom, was once part of a gasworks. Workshop, engineering department and sidings lie west of this, and to the north of the line is the SR station building, with a cafeteria built in sympathetic style and a children's playground beyond. Between station and cafe stand the company offices and a long single-storey building - this was acquired, courtesy of Plessey in Cowes, to house a covered waiting area with tables and chairs, and another room set up as an audio-visual centre. We shall return here later.

On leaving the station we cross the road leading to the village, which lies to the left, and, climbing again at about 1 in 80, the line crosses a short stretch of open country before entering a shallow cutting, with woodland to the south. Beyond an overbridge, the line cuts through Rowlands Wood, and, curves south past the 4-mile post - distances are measured from Ryde. To the south now is open farmland, with the chalk scars of old quarries facing the line from the distant ridge. To the north the land is rougher, as the line bears left into Ashey station.

Ashey is, to quote the railway's leaflet "...an archetypical way-side halt, situated in unspoilt rural surroundings". As, indeed, one suspects it has always been. The original station house, built to the north of the line, is now an attractive private dwelling, and the present platform can be used as a starting point for country walks. The only access is by footpath, and trains stop only on request. It was opened first in 1875 to serve a steeplechase course, now long gone, which lay immediately to the south of the station. BR modernised the station in the early 1960s, only to close it in 1966!

Now the line curves north, climbing again - a short way beyond the platform is the summit of this section. A steep descent follows, near the foot of which is 'long arch', a rather longer than usual overbridge which carries, at an acute angle, a minor road between Ashey and Ryde. A straight section follows, with grazing land to both sides, as on a steadily-falling gradient we curve left and draw up at the platform of Smallbrook Junction.

This was opened, officially on 20th July 1991 and to the public the next day, as an interchange point with BR's Island Line. The platform is timber, at a higher level than the Network SouthEast one, and a ramp connects the two. There is no regular physical rail connection between the systems, but the IoWSR track can be slewed to a junction if necessary. The groundframe comes partly from Whitwell signalbox, on the Ventnor West branch, and two listed buildings from Brading have been acquired for possible use here. As with Ashey, the station has no road access. There isn't even a footpath leading here - the trains use the only way in.

The railway's school operation is one which came as something of a surprise, though I cannot really think why it should. It has developed over the years, and now forms a substantial part of the railway's business, primarily in mid-week, which is in any case the time when trains are often more lightly loaded. The organisation of the parties has changed over the years too - at one time they were split into smaller groups and given over to four or so guides, who would talk to each group in turn. This presented several problems - it was

Right Ex-LSWR O2 class 0-4-4T No.24 Calbourne leaves Haven Street en route for Wootton, 3rd September 1991.

'manpower-intensive', not all the guides were able to hold their audience as effectively as others, and, of course, if it rained everyone got wet. So when the 'Plessey' building became available it seemed the obvious answer. Not only does it provide covered accommodation for the children at lunch time, but the audio-visual facility takes a great deal of weight off the guides' shoulders. One twenty-minute presentation, followed by a question and answer session now suffices for all the previous guides' talks in a much clearer way, and seems to go down better with the children too.

"Several teachers," Pat Kitcher, one of the duty-guides told me, "have said how glad they are that the presentation is of slides rather than a video." Children, it seems, are now so used to videos, that they often switch off mentally on being presented with yet another one - slides, apparently, are something a little different, and hold their attention better. Pat herself has a father-in-law and husband Kevin working on the line, and their son and daughter are now old enough to do the same. A local television station recently celebrated their three-generation service.

The Railway's audio-visual show traces, briefly, the line's history, and goes on to explain, with a professional commentary by a member employed in local radio, how the preservation group came to be formed and to grow. Many aspects of railway work are touched on, and the story of the extension to Smallbrook is told. It is a still-developing story, of course, and Pat pointed out that it would need updating fairly shortly.

"Things have moved on since we got to Smallbrook," she remarked.

The question and answer session was lively during my visit, once the initial ice had been broken.

"We are frequently surprised how deep some of the children's' questions go," said Pat. "It certainly keeps us on our toes - which is how it should be."

Undoubtedly the children I saw during my visit enjoyed themselves, but conversations with both teachers and children left me with a very distinct feeling that the children with teachers who prepared them beforehand about what to expect and look for got a great deal more from their visit than others. The Railway is offering an

Left Austerity 0-6-0ST No.198 Royal Engineer *on a west-bound train between Smallbrook Junction and Ashey, September 1994.*

important service here - in my view it works well and is to be thoroughly applauded.

Where then, does the Railway go from here? To Ryde, perhaps, but that depends on others. There are those who maintain that the line is at present a comfortable length for its facilities, and one cannot argue with this. On the other hand, in such a situation it would become very easy to stagnate, which would be a shame. So what about an extension to Newport.

Terry Hastings paused, choosing his words carefully.

"We have had an approach," he said. "The County Council is interested in a tourist facility at Newport Harbour, and it could be that a steam railway might be a useful part of that. Don't get me wrong, we are still, as of May 1994, no further than the talking stage. It's no more, yet, than a possibility."

"But an exciting one," I suggested.

Terry grinned, and he didn't disagree.

Below *No.W8* Freshwater *seems eager to escape from Haven Street with its train for Smallbrook Junction on 27th September 1994.*

Berwyn Belle

LLANGOLLEN RAILWAY
Llangollen - Glyndyfrdwy

"It is estimated that a preserved steam line at Llangollen would attract more than 100,000 visitors a year. If the proposal is adopted it would provide an operating site for the Flint & Deeside Railway Preservation Society".

So ran an item in the December 1974 issue of *Railway World*, no doubt prompted by a press release from the Society. No mention of Llangollen in the Society's name, you notice. What had happened was that a group of railway enthusiast habitues of the Royal Oak in Flint had got together in 1972, seven years after the line between Ruabon and the Welsh coast at Barmouth had closed and been lifted, and decided that it would be nice to preserve steam on a branch line in North Wales. The Group had no specific site in mind to begin with. Various other trackbeds (the Mold and Dyserth branches, for instance), were discarded before Llangollen was considered, but that consideration resulted in the news item with which this essay began.

A locomotive was stored at a site in Prestatyn, and a first open day on the site at Llangollen station was held on 13th September 1975. It drew 1,500 visitors, a very encouraging beginning, and a plan evolved to develop the line from Llangollen to Berwyn (pronounced Be-roo-in) - a distance of about 1.5 miles. In the autumn of the next year the Society again used the pages of *Railway World*, this time to encourage supporters to buy lengths of track, at £1 a foot. Clearly the project was on its way.

And we, too, are way ahead of the story. Why and how was the railway there in the first place? Well, put very simply, the Great Western Railway wanted its own route to the North Wales coast. The London & North Western had, as it were, cornered the north coast and had a tentacle down towards Swansea via the Central Wales line. The Cambrian Railways had the Mid-Wales route between Shrewsbury and Aberystwyth, and

Left *GWR-design Manor class 4-6-0 No. 7822* Foxcote Manor *crosses the Dee bridge with an up passenger train in May 1990.*

Llangollen Railway

The Station, Abbey Road, Llangollen,
Clwyd, LL20 8SN.
Tel. 01978 860979/890951(tt)

Route Llangollen - Glyndyfrdwy (5.25 miles)
Gauge Standard
Open Please telephone for details.

The Great Western Railway wanted an independent route to the Welsh coast, so in 1860 it backed the Llangollen & Corwen Railway company, which was to extend the branch already being built to Llangollen from the GWR's line at Ruabon. Opened in 1865, it was never, perhaps, quite the money-spinner which the GWR had hoped for, but it struggled on until BR closed it in 1968. After a while a preservation society formed in North Wales during the early 1970s found a home at Llangollen in 1975. The main problem at that time was a bridge across the river Dee, but this obstacle was passed in 1982, and since then steady progress has been made towards the ultimate goal at Corwen. The railway uses ex-BR Mark 1 coaches and has a varied collection of steam and diesel locomotives to pull them. Big engines visit regularly, and Llangollen is one of several centres where engine-driving courses can be enjoyed.

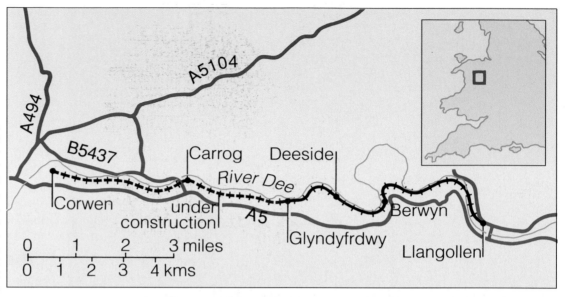

Right Ex-LMS 4F class 0-6-0 No.4422, a visitor from the Cheddleton Railway Centre of the North Staffordshire Railway, enters Glyndyfrdwy with a train from Llangollen on 7th August 1994.

Far right Ex-BR Class 4MT Standard 2-6-0 No. 76079 passes Deeside Halt en route to Llangollen, 12th April 1993.

northwards along the coast to Pwllheli. So the GWR supported an independent company called the Vale of Llangollen Railway, which was to build a line from Ruabon to Llangollen.

This opened on 1st December 1861, worked, of course, by the Great Western Railway, but even before then an extension, the Llangollen & Corwen Railway had been incorporated - on 6th August 1860 - for 9.5 miles of railway between the named towns. The line's Engineer was Henry Robertson, MP. He lived near Wrexham, where he had colliery interests, and he had engineered several Welsh railways, among them the Central Wales line just mentioned. The contractor responsible for building the railway was the well-known and greatly-respected Thomas Brassey, here working in partnership with a man called William Field. Brassey too was fairly local, having been born at Bulkeley Manor near Chester. His railway interests spread a good deal wider than Robertson's, however, and a bust to his memory now stands in Chester Cathedral.

The only significant engineering problem on the section was a 689-yard long tunnel about two miles from Llangollen, which was made as a single-track bore on a curve. It was, (and still is) approached on a gradient of 1 in 80, and presumably the justification for the cost of the tunnel was the possibly even greater sum resulting from following the river's enormous loop to the north here. The line opened between Llangollen and Corwen on 1st May 1865.

The line, eventually extended past Bala to the coast, served a useful purpose though it is doubtful whether it ever realised its full potential in GWR eyes. There was too much competition from other lines, and in due course Dr Beeching, in his infamous report, recommended its closure. This was fixed for mid-January 1965, but fate was to take a hand before that. On 12th December 1964 a bridge was washed away at Llandderfyl, near Bala, and services between Llangollen Goods Junction and Bala were never resumed. The Ruabon-Llangollen spur closed to passengers on the official day, 18th January 1965, and goods traffic continued between Ruabon and Llangollen Goods Junction until 1st April 1968. The track was lifted soon afterwards, and the trackbed sold to the local authority.

Left No.7822 Foxcote Manor *bursts from Berwyn tunnel with a Deeside Halt train on 13th May 1990.*

Seven years later the preservationists took a hand, when on 1st July 1975 the new Society took over Llangollen station. It had but two engines then. One, a 4-wheeled diesel, was named *Eliseg* on that first open day. The other, a 0-6-0 saddletank built by Kitson's in 1932, had arrived at the Society's temporary Prestatyn site on 16th November 1973 from the British Leyland factory at Longbridge, where it had been named *Austin 1*. This engine was to take responsibility for all the early work. It returned to service on 22nd August 1985 after a major overhaul, and was named *Burtonwood Brewer*, for the company which had sponsored the repairs. It remains on indefinite loan.

In 1977 the Flint & Deeside RPS became the Llangollen Railway Society, which was, in all fairness, a more accurate description of its activities. Discussions got under way with Glyndwr District Council, with a view to obtaining the trackbed through to Corwen, and it was hoped that a quarter of a mile of track could be laid during the year, using redundant rail from Brymbo Steelworks and other sources. The station at Llangollen, though run-down, was in reasonable condition and set on both a prime site near the centre of the town and a gorgeous spot beside the

Below No. 7822. Foxcote Manor again, this time making a stately departure from Llangollen's long No.1 platform with an up train on 13th May 1990. This was the first summer in which Llangollen Railway passenger trains could run through the Berwyn tunnel.

River Dee - indeed, part of the down platform is cantilevered above it.

Open days continued, but things moved slowly at first. It was hoped to run a service during the International Eisteddfod at Llangollen during 1979, but the Light Railway Order was not received in time. Major Olver inspected the line on 13th September, and the draft LRO was approved by the Department of Transport in 1980: in that year too a 20-year lease was taken on the trackbed to Carrog (8.75 miles) and the goods yard at Llangollen. Then, on 26th July 1981, the first passenger train from Llangollen for 16 years left the platform. It ran for half a mile over relaid track as far as Ffordd Junction, the entry to the goods yard, where the goods shed was now in use by the Society. Trains were pulled by *Burtonwood Brewer*, and 700 people travelled during the day. An official opening was held the next year, and by the end of the 1982 season the line had been extended a further quarter mile to Pentre Felin, where it was planned to build a run-round loop.

This was the limit of things for some time, at least so far as the public was concerned. Beyond Pentre Felin the bridge across the Dee was in poor condition, and estimates put the cost of righting it at £30,000. While the abutments were sound enough the decking and track-supporting timbers had deteriorated. Appeals were launched: Clwyd County Council, Glyndwr District Council, the Welsh Tourist Board and the Prince of Wales Grant Fund all chipped in with grants or loans, and the work of restoring the bridge, and opening up the line to Berwyn went steadily on.

Bad weather delayed work on the bridge, but by the autumn of 1985 track had been laid into Berwyn station, and the first train ran for clearance tests on 29th June - it was hauled by 7298, Derek Foster's LMS 0-6-0 tank engine, which had reached Llangollen from Southport in 1983, officially for 12 months. It remained to give invaluable service until 1988 before moving to Bury, but has been back at Llangollen since June 1991. This first train however carried visitors only as far as Pentre Felin, because the Inspector had not yet cleared the Dee Bridge for passenger use. The first public train to Berwyn ran on 19th October, using a diesel unit, but *Burtonwood Brewer* did bring a steam train over on opening day - a demonstration freight. More than 23,000 visitors travelled that year, making it, by 40 per cent, the most successful season so far. Steam

for passengers across the bridge was sanctioned on 1st December, in time for the 'Santa Specials', and daily services were run throughout the following summer.

A Manpower Services Commission party began work on platforms and station at Llangollen in October 1986, and during the winter of 1986/7 the track was re-sleepered and upgraded. A 'Schools' week was introduced around this time, and these, to begin with, were a great success. No formal education service was offered, but a tour of the railway was given, from which most benefit was gained by parties who had been given some sort of pre-visit guidance as to what to look for. But as funding cuts began to bite, the number of parties fell away, and the idea was discontinued in this more formal form. The facility remains available, however, for schools interested in using it.

During October 1986 the railway held its first 'Thomas the Tank Engine' weekend. The events were repeated, but that of 1988 was marred, not only by appalling weather but also by some sick-minded person (perhaps sickened by the weather) who broke into the station that night and made off with £4,000-worth of takings. He was caught, and though the money was never recovered directly, a 'Thomas to the Rescue' re-run of the weekend recouped it. The railway seems to have been lucky in this respect - after a more recent break-in, when about £5,000-worth of goods from the shop were taken, the getaway van was stopped a few miles down the road towards Ruabon for a routine police check and the stolen items recovered before the railway knew it had lost them...

Also in 1988 the signalbox at Llangollen Goods Junction (Ffordd Junction) was completed - it was rebuilt to the original Great Western design, using a lever frame from Ruabon Middle Box, and steps, roof and windows from Green Lane, on the Chester to Wrexham line. During excavations for the foundations of the box a quantity of blue engineering bricks was found, which together with some 'Ruabon reds' were incorporated in the base.

Having reached Berwyn and spent a little time consolidating, the next target was about midway between there and Glyndyfrdwy, the next station. A loop and platform would be built in meadows beside the river, a temporary terminus while the line was pushed on to Glyndyfrdwy - say Glin-duh-vruh-dui - usually known

Right *Ex-BR Standard 4 2-6-0 No.76079 brings a mixed freight across the Dee bridge on 2nd November 1992.*

Above Ex-LMS locomotives at Llangollen on 2nd April 1993 - to the left MR-design 0-6-0T No.47298 on a short mixed freight passes ex-LMS Stanier 5MT class 4-6-0 No.44806 standing light at platform 2.

track inside the tunnel, but promised to re-inspect it before Easter. On Good Friday, 13th April 1990, the first public train steamed into Deeside Halt. An official opening by the President of the Society, the Duke of Westminster, was held on 16th June, and 3,500 visitors came to the railway during that weekend.

Funding for the extension to Glyn was now in place. There was a grant of £48,000 from the Welsh Development Agency, a similar amount from the Welsh Tourist Board, and low-interest loans amounting to another £41,000. By July 1,000 yards of track had been laid, and completion was targeted for September 1991. This time the schedule was to over-run slightly, but a final 'gold' fishplate was fitted on 28th March 1992. Major Olver made his inspection in early April and public trains began running on 17th of the month.

Now Corwen beckons. The Welsh Office has approved an access route across a promised by-pass, should it be built, and a site for the station and a plan for crossing the by-pass have already been worked out. Meanwhile the target is Carrog, a station which is still substantially in its original state. On 1st March 1993 a share issue for £500,000 was launched: within three weeks £100,000 had been raised, and a Cheshire firm had donated a mile of track. By July the tally was £190,000, and it was said that if another £30,000 was forthcoming by the end of the year the railway would press ahead with a new shed at Llangollen. It was, and it has - the tally in September 1994 was around £227,000, and building was under way.

The 'Llangollen' has come a long way since its early days, when, says Bill Shakespeare, Chairman of the Society, the vast majority of its income was raised by the sales of waste paper.

"We got as much as £2,000 a year, sometimes," he remarked, a nostalgic gleam twinkling in his eye.

Now membership stands at about 1,700, and the railway has around a dozen paid employees. These are supplemented by about ten per cent of the total membership, though this figure tends to vary in accordance with what projects happen to be ongoing at the time. In 1993 passenger figures recovered to 73,000 after a dip in the previous year, and Bill feels there is potential for 150,000. When I looked quizzical, he grinned.

"Well, maybe that's optimistic" he admitted, "but I really do believe we have the potential, and with the right marketing we could do it, I'm sure."

as Glyn for short! An MSC grant boosted this greatly, and a 48-man team set to work, backed by finance which covered work on the tunnel, clearance, fencing and platform construction. Trains were expected to begin running at Easter 1990, subject, of course, to the usual Ministerial approval.

To most people this was a pretty optimistic forecast, but the Railway Society's faith was not misplaced. The loop at Deeside was completed in August 1989, and the team began to work east towards the then railhead between Berwyn and the tunnel. The final rails were laid on 9th December 1989, a month ahead of schedule, 1.5 miles of track having been laid in five months, including the tunnel. Ballasting and finishing remained, and clearance trials were carried out with No.7828, *Odney Manor*, on 6th January. The Inspector came on 2nd March 1990 - he made recommendations about the alignment and cant of the

There can be few lines more scenic than the Llangollen Railway. The journey begins beside the Dee in a station that, for a town of its size, has incredibly long platforms. The reason, of course, was the excursion traffic which the Great Western expected here - no doubt it had some, but even the International Eisteddfod did not start until after the Second World War, so the GW would have gained little benefit from that. The locomotive will no doubt be taking water from the tower at the top end of the down platform - that is the one nearest the river, even though the slope is actually up...

On the opposite side, at the eastern end of the platform, is the original Llangollen signalbox, now leaking no longer, but restored and recommissioned on 29th June 1991. It may well be that this signalbox actually sees more service now than it did in BR days, for at that time it was brought into service only to cope with excursion traffic, and so spent most of the time switched out.

The start from here is not easy, being on a right-hand curve and a gradient of 1 in 110. As we head westwards beneath the bridge at the platform end, the old goods yard is atop the cutting on the right, behind the carriages which presently form the volunteer quarters. Now we pass a line of carriage stock stabled on our right, at our level. Beyond them it appears that the goods yard has been coming down to meet us - not so: the yard is level and we have climbed to meet it! Llangollen Goods Junction Signal Box is passed on the left, and now the line is almost on a par with the Llangollen Canal, which, half a mile ago, was high above us.

Railway, canal and road all run close together at this point, and soon we reach the spot that, back in 1982, was the limit of operations - Pentre Felin. The sidings here hold the Railway's spare stock in varying stages of decrepitude, but there is limited time to admire it as the line bears away left and crosses the Dee Bridge. This is the closest we have come to the river since leaving the station, and because of the woods now on both sides of the track, we catch only glimpses of it. It can usually be heard though, even above the sound of the engine, and particularly after heavy rain.

Beyond the bridge the gradient has increased to 1 in 80, and this will be maintained for more than a mile, past Berwyn station, where the river comes close beneath the right-hand side as our train draws into the platform. Opposite, and lower, linked to the road and railway by a

suspension bridge, is an hotel, and the story is that the black and white timbering of the station was insisted on by the then owner of the hotel, so that it would complement his own building. Stranger things have happened! To our left now runs the busy A5 trunk road, and I often wonder how many drivers in the mid-80s did something regrettable to their vehicles in surprise at seeing an unexpected train here. Perhaps they still do, though the engines must be a more familiar sight by now.

A fine stone bridge crosses beneath the railway and over the river here. A little further on, and beneath another bridge, this time over the line, will probably be a few more items of rolling stock. This is the site of Berwyn loop (now a siding) where, in the days when Berwyn was used as a terminus, the engine would run round its train. Passengers were decanted on Berwyn platform, and watched their train recede into the distance, a proceeding which, despite comforting assurances from the station staff, occasionally worried some of them. But they soon realised they had time for a cup of tea, and while they enjoyed this the train moved up to the loop, parked with

Below A visitor from the Severn Valley Railway, ex-GWR 45xx class 2-6-2T No.4566 runs into platform 1 at Llangollen with a short freight on 24th August 1992.

a great many precautions - we're talking about a 1 in 80 slope here, remember - and detached the engine, which then ran round, by way of the loop, to the other end. Then it brought the coaches back to the platform, just like a new train, and everyone returned happily back to Llangollen.

Below us on the right-hand side the river winds away to the north, while we continue to climb steeply towards the tunnel. By cutting through the spur of the hill instead of following the river, the railway builders saved something like three miles of distance, not to mention what might have been some embarrassingly sharp curvature. And in any case, since they had already climbed around 200 feet to negotiate the gorge at Berwyn, and needed to retain that height to be at the right level beyond the hill, it would have been both expensive and stupid to waste it.

The 689-yard tunnel is built on a left-hand curve (as we are going) with brickwork facing at each end and partially lined with brickwork inside. The line was never more than single track west of Llangollen, so there was neither need nor intention for a wider bore. At the western end, after a short cutting, the line emerges into a wider valley, the river some distance away on the right, the road away to the left and now much higher. If you know where to look, one of Telford's old tollhouses can be seen beside it, for this was the Holyhead Turnpike that he engineered in 1829.

The gradient eases to 1 in 135 just before the tunnel mouth, and now it levels out completely as the river closes in on the right, more or less at our own level again, and a single field away. Deeside Halt serves no community, though there are a few farmhouses nearby. The platform is placed on the south side of the line and its shelter is one of Brunel's characteristic small-station buildings known as pagodas, on account of their pointed, concave roofs. This particular example comes from the station at Ffestiniog, on the old GW line which ended at the slate mines of Blaenau Ffestiniog. That line branched north from this one at Bala Junction.

The scenery is now less - how can one put it? - aggressive, perhaps. The line continues on the level for a little way beyond the halt and then, for a short distance,

Left Ex-BR Class 4 2-6-0 No. 76079 approaches Llangollen Goods Junction with a down passenger train in April 1993.

actually goes down at 1 in 435. We are heading north-west at this point, the river not far away on the right, and this time, with no gorge to get through, the line is working round a wooded hillside closing on the left. As we curve left the line begins to rise again, at 1 in 290 for a short way and then at 1 in 155, a gradient we shall maintain until we are almost at Glyndyfrdwy. The River Dee comes close beneath the line on the right and veers away again, while the railway itself begins to descend at 1 in 264.

This is to bring it to ground-level for the station at Glyn. A higher line would have meant either a long embankment, or, if it had kept to the contour of the hillside, demolition of property in the village. Both were expensive options, and, in railway engineer's language, best avoided if possible. Glyndyfrdwy station is therefore on the northern edge of the village, just to the west of a level crossing with a lane leading across the river to a road which runs along the opposite side of the valley.

This level crossing was in fact, some little trouble to the new generation of railway builders, because in the time between BR's closure of the line, and the LR's re-

opening, the level of the road had been raised some two feet. The Llangollen's volunteers had two choices. One was to retain the road's present level, and raise both railway and platforms two feet. The other was to return to the original levels and re-grade the road for some distance on either side. In fact the railway elected for a third option, retaining the level crossing at its present height, but allowing the line to descend into the station platform, with a slight hump at the crossing. This means that although the platform top is now slightly higher than before, completed excavation of the previously filled-in trackbed has not been necessary. As required by the lease, the railway resited the children's playground, previously occupying the station area, in the old goods yard on the opposite side of the road. The station building is now a private residence.

Just east of the level crossing stands a handsome signal-box. This came from Leaton, near Shrewsbury, in June 1988, and is fully operational. Each time I go there I enjoy the notice on the gate, which says: "High Speed Trains Pass This Spot". The level crossing gates are a more recent acquisition and are from Rossett, between Chester and

Below GWR-design Manor class No.7822 Foxcote Manor *runs into Berwyn station, high above the river Dee, with an up train on 13th May 1990.*

Wrexham - the Weston Rhyn signalbox has also been obtained, for use at Corwen. The line was approved by the Inspector in April 1992, and the first passenger train for 26 years stopped there on the 8th April that year. The station building came from the motive power depot at Northwich, where it served as the signing on point for train crews. The platform has been resurfaced with facing bricks from Over & Warton in south Cheshire, and the edging stones come from Pen-y-Ffordd, on the Wrexham to Bidston line.

In October 1987 what has become, to some at least, the jewel on the Llangollen Railway's crown was launched - its luxury dining train the Berwyn Belle. There were four more trains in 1988, and the project has snowballed from there. Now, dining trains on preserved railways are by no means unique. Indeed, more than half the railways featured in this book run them, few, it must be said, have such scenery outside the window as diners can enjoy at Llangollen.

Three types of dining train run on the LR: evening dinner trains with a four-course menu, Sunday luncheon trains, and, new in 1993, evening Nightclub Belles, both with three course menus. The Nightclub trains have either a discotheque or live band on board, and accommodation is available for dancing.

In charge are two London-based British Airways colleagues Bob Austin and Dave Wellington. From the start it was felt that only a professional approach to the project would have the right 'feel' for the customers. No good impression is gained from the best meal in the world if it is sloppily served. Airline staff are trained to serve meals quickly and efficiently, and so airline-type training courses were laid on and at once began to pay dividends.

Each train, of course, requires meticulous preparation, and a staff, for a full, 103-cover train, of about 30.

"How many are volunteers?" I asked Ron Owen, one of the stewards. "We couldn't hope to cover a full train," he said. "Usually we have about 60-65 per cent paid staff. Most volunteers just can't afford all the time it takes. I started early this morning, with the preparations, and it may be that I shan't finish until 2am. But that's all right," he added philosophically. "I enjoy it and there isn't another train tomorrow, so I can have a lie-in."

Left Another visitor to Llangollen, this time ex-NER P3 class 0-6-0 No.2392, approaches Deeside Halt on 24th August 1992.

The stock used is not vintage, all having been built between 1955 and 1963, and are therefore all ex-BR. Each dining car, one named *Angharad* and the other *Branwen* will seat 36 people and *Gwenhwyvar*, a brake/dining composite, seats a further 31. *Elen* the kitchen car and *Gwenabwy*, the function car, complete the set. During an evening service the train does two end-to-end trips along the line, pausing now and then at strategic points appropriate to the course of the meal. After arrival back at Llangollen the bar remains open until 11.30, and if one adds the 'putting to bed' time of the train after that it is not difficult to see how Ron's early morning finishes arise. But from the diner's point of view it is an experience not to be missed.

Responsible for booking both evening and lunchtime trains is Robert Jaques, who is also the proprietor of the Bryn Derwen Hotel, visible from the railway just beyond Ffordd Junction. Here I have to declare an interest, for my first meeting with Robert was some years ago when my wife and I turned up to claim our room at the Bryn Derwen, totally unaware that he had anything to do with the railway, or that one can enjoy a meal in his dining room and watch the trains go by at the same time. A short conversation established that I was one of the Awdrys connected with Thomas the Tank Engine.

"Right," Robert announced without further ado. "Your father's books have given my family so much pleasure in past years, I'm going to change your booking and put you in the honeymoon suite!"

Robert now makes sure that there aren't 104 passengers for a 103-seater train, and also books weekends or overnights at Bryn Derwen Hotel which include dinner on the train.

The Llangollen Railway has two major projects, one of which, the share issue for extension to Carrog and then on to Corwen, has been mentioned. A second ambition is to take the line back towards Ruabon. Moves were made in 1988 to protect the trackbed from further development - there has been some overbuilding at the Llangollen end, but this, it is felt, could be covered by a deviation. At Ruabon, terms are settled for a lease of the station yard and bay platform, and Wrexham Maelor Borough Council agreed late in 1988 that a steam centre could be set up there. It remains very much a long-term scheme, but after what the railway has achieved so far, so swiftly, who could say it is just a pipe-dream?.

Poppies on the Heath
NORTH NORFOLK RAILWAY
Sheringham - Holt

"Neath the blue of the sky, in the green of the corn,
It is there that the royal red poppies are born!
Brief days of desire, and long dreams of delight,
They are mine when my Poppy-land cometh in sight."

Those lines, from a poem called *The Garden of Sleep*, were written by Clement Scott, a journalist and poet of the late Victorian era, who visited Sheringham, then a quiet fishing village on the north Norfolk coast. Through Scott's column in the *Daily Telegraph* Sheringham became an 'in' place to visit, and the visitors came by train.

The railway by which they travelled was the Eastern & Midland Railway. It was in June 1887 that this Company opened its extension from Holt to Cromer, but six years later it was in financial difficulties. A new Company was formed, jointly, between the Midland and the Great Northern Railways, and called, to give it its full title, the Midland & Great Northern Joint Railway Company. They shared almost 200 route miles, and the M&GN (or 'Muddle and Get Nowhere' in the eyes of its detractors) served as a useful feeder to the two major systems.

The Company's headquarters was at Melton Constable, where a locomotive works was established: it built a few locomotives of its own, but most of the engines and rolling stock came from a variety of places, sometimes as far away at Manchester or Cornwall. M&GN locomotives were painted a distinctive yellow/brown colour, and this, combined with much polished brasswork, gave them a very dashing appearance.

Before the railway came, Sheringham was somewhat remote, but the new line brought easier access and a new prosperity. 'Sheringham' had acquired something like the name we recognise by 1242 but until 1889 remained a

Left B12 4-6-0 No. 8572 back home on the North Norfolk Railway in early 1995 after a major three and a half year rebuild in Mansfeld locomotive works, Germany.

North Norfolk Railway

Sheringham Station, Sheringham,
Norfolk, NR26 8RA.
Tel. 01263 822045/825449(tt)
Route   Sheringham - Holt (5.25 miles)
Gauge   Standard
Open   Please telephone for details.

The Eastern & Midlands Railway was an amalgamation of three smaller Norfolk companies, which was authorised in 1882. Its line stretched from Kings Lynn to Great Yarmouth, and a branch to Cromer (Beach) was opened in 1887. The company became part of the Midland & Great Northern Joint Railway from 1st July 1893. After the 1923 Grouping the LNER took over working from 1936, and BR closed the system almost entirely in 1959. Preservation began almost at once, and now the line's headquarters is at Sheringham, with its main workshop at the halfway point, Weybourne. Visitors (on the right of the train as it leaves Sheringham) should see magnificent views towards the coast, and there is wilder country on Kelling Heath as the line climbs steeply towards Holt. Small engines run the line for the most part, and ex-BR carriages form the trains. This much-filmed railway captures the branch line atmosphere well, and a round trip will take just over an hour.

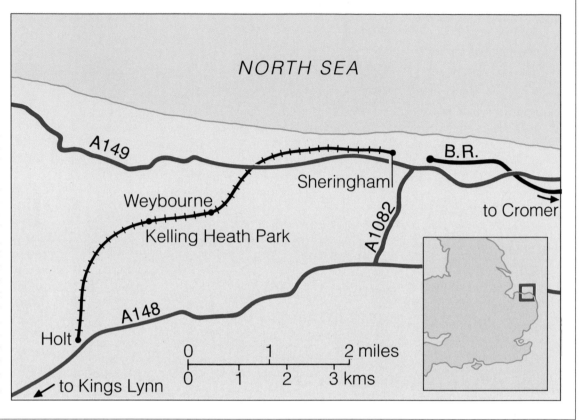

small village set in a cleft in the cliff, whose inhabitants made their living from fishing. For 300 years the only access to the beach was by a flight of steps, but as, during the late 19th century, the fishing industry grew and the railway arrived, the fisherfolk began offering lodging to visitors. By 1898 two large hotels had opened, and by 1911 the population was 3,768, more than double the 1,490 it had been in 1891. 1911 was a peak year - Sheringham regularly booked more rail passengers than Cromer Beach - when 89,702 travelled, 184 per cent more than Cromer.

Most of the M&GN was laid with single track, which undoubtedly led to slow journey times. In 1936 the LMS (as successor to the Midland) passed its share of responsibility for the line to the LNER (succeeding the Great Northern), which worked it simply as a branch. This did not help its prospects. Many of the towns served by the old M&GN system were served also by ex-Great Eastern stations, and slow journey times did it no favours

either. On 28th February 1959 most of the M&GN system closed. The stretch which is the subject of this essay survived a little longer than the rest, as a branch between Melton Constable and Cromer, but all that ceased on 4th April 1964.

Now almost the whole of the Midland & Great Northern system lies either abandoned or used by roads to bypass towns. Only here, on the north Norfolk coast between Holt and Cromer, on what must have been one of its most scenic sections, does the railway survive. Thanks to the volunteers of the North Norfolk Railway, steam still operates between Sheringham and Holt.

Their story begins round about 1959. An absurd first plan was to re-open the entire system, while a less absurd but still over-ambitious second plan was to re-open 22 miles of track between North Walsham Town and Salisbury Road, Great Yarmouth. More modest proposals were to restore services between either North Walsham and Aylsham North or a three-mile section between Melton Constable and Hindolvestone. Neither however had a perceived 'centre' nor anything other than restricted tourist potential, at least then. At this point came publication of the Beeching Report. British Railways at once proposed abandonment of the services between Melton and Cromer - for the intending preservationists it was, you might say, just what the Doctor ordered.

Public support was obtained, and enough funding to buy the line between Sheringham and Weybourne in 1965. Working parties went in, and two engines - both ex-Great Eastern - and a set of carriages arrived. The carriages were of particular historical interest in that, although not directly connected with the M&GN, they had been designed by the LNER's famous Chief Mechanical Engineer, Sir Nigel Gresley for suburban use around London. A single bogie supported each internal carriage-end, thus articulating the set, and since it was a 4-car set, it became known as Quadruple Articulated, or Quad-Art for short.

At first things looked rosy for the railway. Holt signalbox was moved to Weybourne, where, over two weekends, volunteers laid 310 yards of track to form a runround. Signals were bought from the Sutton Bridge to Holbeach section of the old M&GN line, and track came in from Cromer gasworks. That year there was an operating line from Weybourne to a point by the Golf Club Crossing, about a quarter of a mile short of Sheringham station. Access to the station was still hoped for, but, enthusiasm notwithstanding, it became even harder to make ends meet. And since one of the criteria for granting a Light Railway Order is, very properly, safety, the Department of the Environment needed convincing that safety standards could be maintained.

The Spring bank holiday weekend drew a crowd of 2,000 to Sheringham station to witness the first steaming of ex-Great Eastern Class J15 0-6-0 No.65462. The weather during the winter of 1968/9 was bleak, but work continued, and the poet John Betjeman became the Society's first president. Then, on 1st July 1969 the North Norfolk Railway was floated as a Public Company, the first of the preservation societies to be so.

It proved to be the turning point, and progress then became both rapid and permanent. The Light Railway Order was granted to BR (who had applied on the NNR's behalf) in March 1973, and was transferred to the

preservation society early in 1976, the line then being passed for passenger traffic, subject to inspection. Fare-paying passengers were actually carried for the first time, under a special arrangement with BR, during the summer of 1975, 8,000 of them in August alone. A total of 288 trains were timetabled for the following year on 55 operating days, and in 22nd October 1977 a special train was worked to mark the first full season of operation. In 1980 a record of 110,000 passengers was carried, and the North Norfolk Railway could be said to be truly launched.

In 1981 track materials were bought for an extension westwards over the Kelling Heath to a new terminus at Holt - the site of the old station was now covered by a bypass. It was expected that tracklaying would begin in 1982, and the first panel was laid on 21st October that year. Formal opening of the first stage, to Kelling Camp Halt, was on 17th September 1983, when the first arrival was railbus No.E79960. Passengers had, in fact, been using the halt since 28th August.

Above Ex-GNR N2 class, bearing its BR No.69523 during a visit to the North Norfolk Railway during 1994. The locomotive is here seen taking water at Sheringham on 4th September.

line is virtually nil. The unique Quad-Art set lies here, in the open and getting more expensive to save by the day. There is, I was told, some hope of secure accommodation for these coaches, but much else needs shelter no less. There is, perhaps, an argument that funding for this and visitor facilities might be more beneficial.

During the second day of my visit I spent a damp and misty, but very enjoyable few hours as assistant stationmaster at Holt. Business was steady rather then brisk, as might be expected in such weather, coming mainly in 15-minutes or so rushes prior to the departure of each train. I very quickly learned that it is essential to keep one's wits about one at all times, and that a cheerful 'good morning' to a visitor can make all the difference between a £5 fare in the cashbox and a gravel-scattering departure. Several school parties travelled that day, all

Below Ex-GNR J52 class 0-6-0ST No.1247 at Sheringham with a Holt train on 19th September 1993. Ex-LMS 0-6-0T No.47383 was also a visitor, from the Severn Valley Railway.

pre-booked from Sheringham, but for short periods they made the station nicely full. My 'boss' was Fred Stone, a small, bewhiskered 77-year-old, who travels from Norwich four days a week to do his voluntary duty at the station, and obviously enjoys every minute of it. A railway modeller when at home, he kept me well-entertained during quieter periods with tales of this and his army service in South Wales.

The North Norfolk has always, despite its steep gradients, been seen as a small-engine line. At the beginning only small engines were needed anyway, and some which worked here in the early days have moved away to other lines. Two engines which have been here from the start, one of them in service, and the other by the time you read this are an ex-Great Eastern Class J15 0-6-0 and an LNER Class B12 4-6-0. The former was retubed in 1969 and was the mainstay of the line in its early days. It was built at Stratford (London) in 1912 to a design of James Worsdell, and is the only surviving example of a type which worked widely throughout East Anglia. It has had several guises during its time in North Norfolk and is (1994) involved in a major overhaul.

The B12 is also unique. Not so many of them were built as of Class J15, but it is an important engine, built in Manchester for the LNER during 1928 by Beyer Peacock - who also, incidentally, built engines for the M&GN, so it is not, perhaps, a total stranger here. The restoration of this engine has been a very long-term project which should shortly come to a conclusion, and whose imminent return was causing some excitement among members. The plan of campaign, as outlined to me in July 1994, was to use the engine in Norfolk for two years, and then to send it out to other railways as an ambassador for its home line.

The large collection of rolling stock, both goods and passenger, vintage and modern, is far too long to list here, but mention should be made in particular of the Gresley Buffet car No.51769 (or E9128E under the LNER's 1946 renumbering), built in York in 1937. This was acquired by the M&GNRS in 1977, the year of its withdrawal by BR, and arrived in Weybourne at once. It took 11 years to restore it and £20,000, but resplendent in new Brazilian teak it was awarded the ARPS award for 1988, jointly, and a Scania award also. A second Gresley coach, also smartly restored, stands in Sheringham platform, fitted with display boards and audio-visual equipment as an information point.

The most recent rolling stock acquisition is some much-needed accommodation for volunteers in the shape of a Mk 3A sleeping-car, in good condition and only 13 years old. There was accommodation before, of course, but as General Manager David Madden, writing in *Joint Line* points out, the old LMS design sleeping car used for the last 14 years is well past its 'sell by' date. The new vehicle is due to go into use in the 1995 New Year

The main event in the immediate future will be the return of the B12. Also required is a proper station building at Holt. Progress has recently been made in the transfer of the ticket office from a grounded GER carriage body to a large portacabin, which, and by the time you read this, will have been fitted up to look rather more like a station building than it presently does. But a proper station is the aim, and there is also, of course, the museum scheme. Sheringham station is scheduled for attention too, where it is hoped to re-erect the missing buildings and canopies on platform 2 - BR removed the originals in 1965 in order, it claimed, to prevent vandalism.

Can the railway go any further? The guidebook is guarded, but suggests that if the line to Cromer became available the railway "...would seriously consider the possibility of taking it over, though there would be many obstacles to overcome, both physical and financial." Progress beyond Holt is not feasible, because the bypass has taken over the trackbed. As with everything else, much depends on the availability of finance and labour. This part of Norfolk is a little out of the way, and the 'hard core' of regular volunteers is, perhaps as a result, a smaller proportion of the membership than on many other railways.

"Several of our members," remarked Geoff Gowing sadly, "became disillusioned at the slow progress of the B12, and gradually fell away. Our hope is that when the engine comes back later this year we shall have a very welcome boost in membership, and consequently in the number of volunteers available."

He is probably right. Whatever happens, I feel sure that all visitors will be made as welcome as I was and will enjoy, as much as I did, their visit to the North Norfolk Railway.

Above *Ex-NER design J72 class 0-6-0T No.69023 approaches Weybourne, the sea glinting in the background, with a train from Sheringham in August 1989.*

Irwell Valley Adventure

EAST LANCASHIRE RAILWAY
Bury - Rawtenstall

There has been a railway along the Irwell valley for a long time now. It is thanks only to a group of dedicated railway enthusiasts and the faith in the project that has been shown by local authorities in Bury, Rawtenstall, Rossendale and Rochdale that it is there still. This local authority commitment was backed by substantial funding, and in 1991 this allowed a small group finally to establish an 8-mile-long railway.

The first rails along the valley were laid by a company originally incorporated (in 1844) as the Manchester, Bury & Rossendale Railway. It did not keep the name for long, because on 3rd August 1846 it absorbed the neighbouring Blackburn, Burnley, Accrington & Colne Extension Railway and became, probably to everyone's relief, simply the East Lancashire Railway Company.

The line was built to serve cotton mills at Ramsbottom, Rawtenstall, Bacup and intermediate points. Contractors for the railway were Pauling & Henfrey, and the first 14 miles from Manchester to Rawtenstall (the mileposts beside the line measure from Manchester Victoria to this day, though through running is now impossible) opened to the public on 28th September 1846. A formal opening had happened three days before. An extension to Newchurch (2 miles) opened two years later, on 27th March 1848, and another 2.5 miles - an extension of the extension, you might say - to Bacup on 1st October 1852.

Bury was the headquarters of the line, and the fine building in the grand classical style erected to house it, was demolished only in the late 1960s. The station, built on the edge of the town, was known simply as Bury at first, but became Bolton Street when a second station, at Knowsley Street, was opened in 1848 by the Lancashire & Yorkshire Railway on its east/west route. Indeed, in

Left Ex-GWR 5205 class 2-8-0T No.5224 storms past Burrs with the 1100 Bury to Rawtenstall train on 29th December 1992.

65

East Lancashire Railway

Bolton Street Station, Bury, Lancashire, BL9 0EY.
Tel. 0161 764 7790

Route	Bury - Rawtenstall (8 miles)
Gauge	Standard
Open	W/e, b/h throughout the year; special events.

The Manchester, Bury & Rossendale Railway was incorporated in 1844 to build a line to serve cotton mills in the Irwell valley. Two years later, after absorbing another company with a long name, it became the East Lancashire Railway. It also opened as far as Rawtenstall that year, extending through to Bacup in 1852. Seven years later the Lancashire & Yorkshire Railway absorbed the ELR, only to be absorbed itself, prior to the 1923 Grouping, by the London & North Western Railway. Though BR's passsenger service to Rawtenstall ceased in 1972, the freight traffic survived until 1980. Preservation moves began as early as 1969, but it took some time for the Society to establish itself: in the last few years, however, the railway has grown rapidly, thanks largely to local council funding, and now has an attractive 8-mile run through the surprisingly scenic Irwell valley. Big engines and ex-BR carriages convey the passengers through restored or rebuilt stations, and at the Bury end is an extensive workshop based in an ex-BR electric train depot. An extension eastwards from Bury to a link with the national railway system near Heywood is in hand.

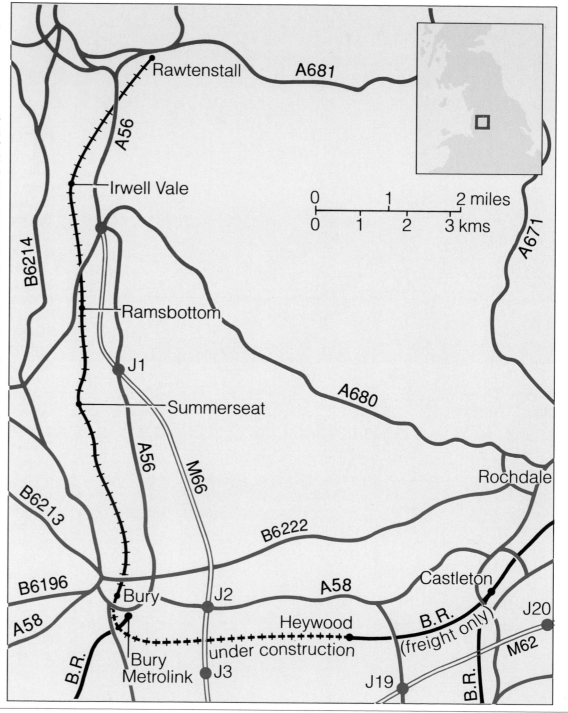

Far right Ex-LNER A3 class 4-6-2 No.4472 Flying Scotsman *hurries past Elwood Bridge heading the 0900 Bury-Rawtenstall train in February 1993.*

Far right Ex-LMS 5MT class 2-6-0 No.42765 heads past Irwell Vale towards Rawtenstall with a mixed freight on 22nd February 1994.

1859, it was the Lancashire & Yorkshire which absorbed the East Lancashire Railway, in whose hands it remained until 1922, when the L&Y became part of the London & North Western Railway in preparation for the Grouping of the following year.

After the Second World War trade along the valley declined - the Accrington branch and the Rawtenstall-Bacup extension closed on 5th December 1966, and the passenger service between Bury and Rawtenstall ceased completely on 5th June 1972. A preservation project was first suggested when the Accrington branch closed, but BR offered it for sale only a fortnight before closure, when there was no hope of raising the purchase price in the time available, and refused to lease it. Disheartened and frustrated, the Society lost many members. Those who remained decided to concentrate their efforts on establishing a museum at Bury. Activity began in the 1846 Castlecroft goods yard and shed near Bolton Street, and Bury Transport Museum opened on 17th August 1969.

Hopes of opening a railway had not evaporated completely however, for the *Railway World* of October 1969 reported that the East Lancashire Railway Preservation Society was negotiating with BR and the Ministry of Transport "...to purchase and operate the 3.5 miles of line between Haslingden Grane Road and Stubbins Junction near Ramsbottom." In fact there were to be no fewer than seven years of protracted negotiations, planning procedures and meetings, and when the dust had settled it was not the Haslingden-Stubbins section that was saved anyway!

BR withdrew its freight service from the Rawtenstall branch on 4th December 1980. The ELRPS at first planned to take over in 18 months, but, reported *Railway World* in February 1981, was now hoping to be able to run trains later that year. The Museum was well-established and local authorities had begun to show an interested in creating a linear park along the valley. Money began to flow, and by 1987 Bury and Rossendale Councils together with Lancashire County Council and the Greater Manchester Council had contributed in excess of £1 million. The East Lancashire Railway is the first to be opened as a direct result of financial commitment by local councils, and the amount of this commitment makes the project unique.

The railway is controlled by a Trust of 12 people - four from each of the interested Borough Councils and four from the railway. These Councils see the leisure aspect of the line and area it serves as all-important - they bought the route and track structures, negotiated with grant-giving bodies and on the design of stations to replace those destroyed by BR. A viaduct at Ramsbottom was replaced by embankment at a cost of £53,000, substantial track renewal was needed, along with refencing, and a landslip at Summerseat had to be dealt with. On the credit side it was reported that both tunnels were sound, which must have been a great relief to all concerned.

Land was leased in 1980 to extend the Museum, and was expected that a new shed (cost £20,000) would be completed by the end of the year. There was little hope of a passenger service by that time however. Permission for a dining service was given for the Spring of 1982, "...to test public reaction." It was good, and the work went on. In 1986 a Light Railway Order was obtained, and the Board of Trade's approval was sought some steam workings along the half-mile of track between Bury and Buckley Wells during a 'Steam-Up' arranged for 26th/27th May that year.

Easter 1987 was now the projected date for the opening of the first section of the restored line, between Bury and Summerseat. Crew training began in December 1986, and on 29th January 1987 a press run was made. A sum of £600,000 had been given to the railway by the Department of the Environment, and this paid for corrective work to a landslip at Summerseat, the conversion of Ramsbottom Reservoir viaduct to embankment - the fact that the reservoir had been drained made this possible - for fencing and other drainage work. Strengthening work was also required at Brooksbottom viaduct, and the single track was slewed to the centre to ease some of the stresses.

In the event the proposed Easter opening was postponed twice, first to 6th June and finally to 25th July, when the opening train left Bury at 11am with civic dignitaries and invited guests on board. The event had all the atmosphere of a Victorian railway opening - the Clan Grant pipe-band piped, Morris dancers danced, and 'See the Conquering Hero Comes' was sung, no doubt heroically. The formalities of the day were in charge of (or, as a Victorian newspaper would have put it "were discharged by") the Mayor of Rawtenstall, and a buffet lunch for the invited guests was provided by Bury Council. So many other people came to see what was happening that an extra train had to be provided. Six further

departures were made during the day, which was reckoned to have been a resounding success. By the end of September the railway had carried in excess of 20,000 passengers, probably more than BR's tally for the line over a year, and emphatic vindication, if any were needed, that the East Lancashire Railway was on its way.

The opening train, not to mention all the rest of them on that day, was headed by *Gothenberg*, an ex-Manchester Ship Canal 0-6-0 side-tank engine built by Hudswell Clarke in 1903. She was acquired for the Society shortly after it moved to Bury, in 1972. The other engine was ex-Meaford Power Station No.1, another 0-6-0 side-tank, but much younger, having come from the factory of Robert Stephenson & Hawthorn only in 1950. This locomotive was bought from its American owner and arrived at Bury in 1978; its overhaul was complete by December 1980 in

black livery, though by the time of the opening it had acquired a handsome coat of dark blue.

Another of the locomotive stalwarts of those early days was a Hunslet-built 'Austerity' No.8, dating from 1953. A large number of this type were built for the National Coal Board, and many have found their way onto preserved railways - this particular one came to the railway from Bickershaw Colliery in 1985. Named *Sir Robert Peel*, after the founder of the police force (a native of Bury), this engine was the mainstay of the passenger service during 1988/9.

There were plaudits from the Association of Railway Preservation Societies too, which gave the ELR its 1987 award, for "...arousing, maintaining and developing the enthusiasm of local authorities and local communities, resulting in the opening of an initial four-mile section of

Above *GWR-design Manor class 4-6-0 No. 7828* Odney Manor *leaves Irwell Vale with a Rawtenstall train on 16th January 1994.*

Far left *Ex-LMS Jubilee class 4-6-0 No.45593* Kolhapur *leaves Bolton Street tunnel, Bury, with a northbound train on 30th August 1993.*

the line from Bury to Ramsbottom".

During January 1990 limestone ballast, 850 tons of it, was laid at Rawtenstall, and the final stretch of line was officially inspected during the month. The Inspector recommended a delay in opening - signalling was still being installed, and he requested that there should be a proving period before traffic began. An intended Autumn opening was postponed, to allow for complete refurbishment of the line, and the rebuilding of Rawtenstall station was begun during May.

At last, on 27th April 1991 *Gothenberg* and *No.1* were flagged away by the Mayor of Bury, Monty Adler. Scheduled departure time for the 6-coach train of maroon ex-BR Mark 1s had been 11.10am, but actual time was 11.40, *Gothenburg* breaking a celebratory banner as the train left. At the other terminus the Mayor of Rawtenstall, Philip Dunne, unveiled a plaque, and during a speech made at the reception afterwards, described the railway as a project of excellence.

"It has succeeded, and it deserves to go further," he said.

Thirteen years on, my escort round the line was Roy Holt, a regular volunteer who lives in nearby Bolton.

"We've come a long way very fast," he said, "and the trouble is, the faster you run the more people expect. There's been no time to stand still and consolidate, which is maybe a pity, but at least nobody can say that nowt ever happens."

One of Roy's jobs is the 'ELR tour', one of the reasons perhaps why the railway can call on a larger percentage of regular volunteers than most other lines seem to be able to muster, about 400 out of a total membership of around 2,500. With only a single member of staff paid by the railway - four others are funded by other means - one suspects they need all the volunteers they can get. Another reason, I suggested, for the higher than average turnout rate might be that there were still plenty of projects on the line for the volunteers to get interested in. Projects galore, in fact, the only limits (presumably) being funding and time. The signalbox at Bury, for instance, will be fitted out with a 65-lever frame and will then control the Bury end from the engine shed to a point 750 yards north of the station, and the whole of the Heywood branch. A 15in gauge locomotive is also being built, and it proposed that this will run between the station at Bury and the shed, where a viewing gallery is to be installed. The shed from

Dinting is to be erected on an area near the big running shed, a boiler shop has been suggested...

In the shed/workshop is a very well equipped set-up which can cope with almost anything that is thrown at it. Roy took great delight in pointing out that despite various lives as electric depot, dmu depot and other things, it had now been returned to its original ELR use as a steam locomotive workshop. The Lancashire & Yorkshire Railway, had considered putting its locomotive works at Bury until the claims of Horwich decreed otherwise, and this building would, no doubt have been part of it. The works never came, but this structure, now owned by the new ELR, survives and has 'listed' status. It also serves as home, for the time being, for several items from the National Railway Museum, another reason why a viewing gallery is thought necessary.

The second station in Bury was Knowsley Street, which lay on an east/west axis, its line crossing below the ELR just south of Bolton Street and connected to it from the north by a steep spur. The line went to Heywood and Rochdale, and it is this line which the ELR is seeking to revive as a main line connection to its own metals on one hand and as a potentially valuable freight outlet on the

Far left GWR-design Manor class 4-6-0 No. 7828 Odney Manor *and ex-SR Battle of Britain class 4-6-2 No.34072* 257 Squadron *storm north past Burrs on 26th January 1992.*

Below Ex-LMS 4F class 0-6-0 No.44311 brings a northbound passenger train past Elwood Bridge on 28th December 1992.

other. Because the Manchester Metro now enters Bury just to the east of Bolton Street, and because a crossing of the two lines on the level would not be permissible, the ELR has had to climb steeply to a new bridge across the Metro before falling away on the far side. As originally planned, the gradient to this bridge from the west was to have been 1 in 27, but by making the summit of the line on the east side of the bridge, it has been possible to reduce this to 1 in 29. With a sharp curve to negotiate too, this will not be the easiest section of line to work, though the sharpest part of the curve does not coincide with the steepest part of the gradient. But if various commercial schemes by traders up the Irwell valley come to fruition, the new link to the main railway system could be an extremely valuable asset to the ELR.

Bolton Street station is, like Loughborough on the Great Central Railway, an island platform approached from the street. It is the only (so far) early BR station to be preserved, the Lancashire & Yorkshire building of 1880 having been destroyed in a fire during 1947. With this in mind, no doubt, the railway has set its 'period' as the BR of the late 1950s, a decision which also makes more logical the large fleet of diesel locomotives which it uses. These are housed and maintained in a large new shed built and equipped in 1989 to the south of the station.

Immediately north of the platform is the short 80-yard Bolton Street tunnel, and beyond it, on the left (west) lies the goods yard and original site of the Museum, set at an acute angle to the railway. The original double track is singled throughout the line, though trains can pass at each terminus and there is a passing loop at Ramsbottom.

Leisure railway it may be, but for the engine and crew it is no holiday, and the climbs are not easy. Almost a mile and a half at 1 in 136 brings the line to Summerseat, at present the first station out, a platform and shelter with a short section of low, original ELR platform at the southern end. To comply with Health & Safety directives, the main platform is to be extended at the northern end, so that this section, though retained, will pass out of use. The down platform (ELR down trains run uphill!) lies opposite, very much overgrown. Just beyond the Summerseat station - whose curious name derives simply from the fact that it was the site of a hut or sheiling used during the summer - are the two tunnels, Brooksbottom (423 yards) and Nuttall (115 yards). Nuttall tunnel has faces carved on the north portal, said to be those of original ELR directors. Both

bores are on a gradient of 1 in 128, with a very short pitch of 1 in 116 just before the former, and the slope eases to 1 in 264 through Ramsbottom station.

Ramsbottom, whose name has nothing what ever to do with sheep, but comes from ramm, an old word for wild garlic, lies four miles away from the start of our journey. Hopes that wood pulp might be brought in by rail to Trinity Paper Mill, which stands opposite the station, have not yet materialised, but staff are optimistic. The 'station accommodation' here was once a ship's container (aka 'the tin hut') but the fine new building was designed by the local authority architects and paid for, in part, by the now defunct Greater Manchester Council. It is a stone building based on the style of the original ELR, and won an Ian Allan Heritage award in 1989. It has a booking office, ladies' and general waiting rooms done out in the authentic two-tone green ELR livery, toilets and a bookshop, together with original-style platform signs and clock. A Lancashire & Yorkshire pattern canopy awaits erection, and the shelter on the up platform - that's the one 'facing' Bury, remember - is reconstituted from a bus shelter, but in the authentic ELR style.

There may be a little trouble in erecting the canopy - which comes from Atherton - here, for various practical reasons, but what also has not yet (August 1994) been decided is whether its entire 120 feet should go on the down side or whether the passengers for Bury should get some benefit from it. It would perhaps be a pity to divide it, yet 120 feet does seem overlong in relation to the size of the building on the down side. The station building has a very pleasing aspect, and it might be a shame to overshadow it too much.

At the north end of the station is a handsomely reconstructed footbridge, which came from Dinting, and a very busy level crossing. There are none of your automatic barriers here - despite the continuous traffic, some of it pretty heavy, it is a traditional gated crossing worked in the traditional way by a gatewheel in the signalbox. A gate-wheel in a signalbox was my introduction to railway operation more years ago than I intend to write down here, and to see this one in regular use was a delight. The box itself has a long lever-frame

Right *A wintry morning, 31st December 1993, as ex-GWR 5205 class 2-8-0T No.5224 brings the 1000 Bury-Rawtenstall train across Brooksbottom viaduct.*

for what is, after all, only a crossing loop, but contains some very sophisticated fail-safe equipment. This allows the signalman to make one mistake, but if he then attempts anything which will compound the error, the whole box switches itself off for two minutes. Two minutes can seem a long time, as Roy demonstrated, and in, say, a busy junction box might be highly inconvenient, but here it seems a very sensible safety measure.

Ramsbottom viaduct once crossed a reservoir. The reservoir had been drained before the Preservation Society came into being, and it was decided that, in the interests of both economy and safety, the viaduct should be converted to an embankment. During 1987 the life-expired cast-iron spans were lifted out and the course of the railway was then infilled.

The general direction of the line as far as Ramsbottom has been north-west, but beyond there it heads north. Stubbins Junction lies half a mile on, at the top of a pitch of 1 in 140. The station site is hard to pick out now, and it is even harder to realise that this was once the important point where the Accrington and Bacup lines diverged. It is another place at which there is a paper mill which might or might not take rail-borne wood-pulp. A steel works hereabouts has also expressed interest in a rail-link, but all will depend, of course, on the extension over the 'ski-slope' towards Heywood.

The ELR is perhaps thankful in retrospect that its line now parts company with the notorious gradients of the Accrington branch. The line runs beside the abandoned trackbed for some time, but even given the gradient on our line (1 in 132) the nearby embankment climbs even more steeply at 1 in 94. After a while ours trends north-east, giving us, through the trees, a brief glimpse of a spectacular stone viaduct across the Irwell - a listed structure but scarcely safe to walk over, let alone carry a train - before the northerly branch is lost to view.

Irwell Vale is built at the site of a closed siding and is a new station, replacing one a short distance further on called, in L&Y and BR days, Ewood Bridge & Edenfield. The contractor who built the station quoted less for the nine-coach platform required than the others who tendered quoted for a six-coach one, and naturally got the job. It has a picnic site behind the small stone shelter, and, now that the local inhabitants have got used to it, they have begun to keep it looking good with flowers and plants from their own gardens.

After two more crossings of the Irwell the site of Ewood Bridge is passed, marked by a L&YR timber goods shed on the down side, which, unusually, replaced a stone building in 1896 and, perhaps even more unusually, survives. A quarry can be seen high on the hill to the right. This was Horncliffe Quarry, and a narrow gauge incline once linked it with the Irwell Valley line. A level-crossing at Townsend Fold crosses another road that has become much busier in recent years, and it is the intention in due course, Roy said, to take the gatewheel equipment from the signalbox at Rawtenstall and transfer it here.

Rawtenstall (which apparently meant originally a 'rough cow pasture') lies some half a mile further on and is likely to remain the terminus of the line at this end, for road improvements have taken much of the trackbed between here and Bacup. The site here is awkward, and a steep gradient was the cause of the Inspector's request for delay - he required that the slope be eased to 1 in 280 through the platform. This meant that the trackbed had to be excavated to an appropriate depth and relevelled. The result is that though the platform is still on the site of the original it is some 18 inches lower. The trains run into a platform on the up side, the only service platform at present. Also on the up side is a bay, and when, as is planned, the platform is extended out to the watercolumn, the bay will be long enough for a 9-coach train, the maximum the railway intends to run.

On the down side of the terminal buffers the platform extends only a few yards, and may, Roy told me, become the start of a 7.25" gauge line back towards Townsend Fold. The new station here is similar in style to that at Ramsbottom, but bigger. It is L-shaped, in stone, and contains a good-sized booking hall and shop, with waiting rooms and toilets facing the platform. A fine stone building nearby was sold by BR before the ELR came into being - a pity, perhaps, for it would have made a superb running shed/museum/showcase for the railway.

The second day of my visit dawned with heavy rain, which did not bode well, for it had already been intimated that my duties would be with the platform staff at Bury. As the first train left I was handed a wide broom and invited to clear some of the puddles from the platform. For a second I had thoughts of elbow-grease and left-

Right *Ex-GWR Castle class 4-6-0 No.5029* Nunney Castle, *passes Burrs on 3rd January 1993.*

handed spanners. They were unworthy, though at that stage sweeping puddles seemed like an act of faith, for some of the clouds scudding eastwards overhead were still grey verging on black. But in fact there was only one more brief shower - right on cue as that first train arrived back, of course!

The ELR uses mainly ex-BR Mark 1 stock, and the toilets in these, together with the watertank for the buffet car on each of the two sets need replenishing with water after each trip. This became my main job for the day. The business end of the long hose, attached at the other end to the watermain, had to be slid on to the carriage inlet pipe, left until the overflow went into action, and then transferred to the next along the train. So it was a question of slip the pipe on - wait for the overflow - move on to the next, avoiding spray as far as possible - make a mental note to remove wristwatch next time - drag hose along a bit further - realise that it won't come because a passenger is standing on it - allow him to board train - give an extra hard tug for the three inches needed to reach the next inlet - wonder why water has stopped flowing - hurry back along platform to repair parted joint in the pipe - complete one train - stand back to wait for next - remember to switch off water in meantime - switch back on at next train's arrival - fail to remember to take off watch - and so on. Actually, once one did take off one's watch, the spray was really no problem - during the shower one could have got no wetter, and it was pleasantly cooling when the sun came out!

Frank was my mentor during the day, and armed with a rubbish bag and supplies of paper towels and toilet rolls we boarded the last departure from Bury. During the trip to Ramsbottom we checked that all the toilets were properly supplied, and once there I transferred to the up train which we crossed at that point, and performed a similar task on that. Once back at Bury, we waited until the set had been stabled in the opposite platform, and then Stuart, the third member of the staff on the day, and I, went through it with brushes, dustpans and binliners. Frank meanwhile went on to Rawtenstall with the down train, and would clean that set as far as he could during the journey back to Bury.

Left Ex-GWR 5205 class 2-8-0T No.5224 with a northbound train, passes between the Nuttall tunnels on 3rd May 1993.

Cleaning was finished before the final arrival of the day, and just as this was being stabled a van arrived from the local cash and carry with buffet supplies of cans, soft drinks, sweets and other comestibles for the next goodness knows how long! All this first required transfer from the van to the far platform, then a portage across the tracks to our platform, where we loaded (in railway terms I suspect we overloaded) a luggage trolley. This was wheeled to the door of the coach used as a store, and yet another handling got most of the stock where it was needed, and the 'other supplies' were wheeled elsewhere for restaurant car use. I drove from the car-park at 6.35pm after a nine-hour day - the buffet car staff and others would probably there for some time longer yet!

Volunteer staff undoubtedly make huge sacrifices for the railway they serve, not simply in terms of hours, but because a willing horse is always perceived as being willing to carry a little more. For some a time comes when enough is more than enough, which may be one reason why many fight shy of volunteering, feeling unable to give the commitment they see others giving. In truth they really need have no fear - those who run the railway are only too aware of the pressures, and know that if they could only call on a larger number of volunteers everyone would be able to enjoy fewer calls on their time. By far the best way is to decide beforehand what sort of commitment one is prepared to offer: I have never known a management to turn down help, however small it seems.

The East Lancashire Railway is run by more than 99 per cent volunteered labour, and, even leaving aside all the financial backing it has had from local boroughs, is a very remarkable achievement of which the members have every reason to feel proud. There is, it seems, only one small regret.

"We'd like to be known as the 'Friendly Line', Roy told me, "but that title has already been used by the Welshpool people." He grinned and went on: "When we showed a party from the W&L round a few weeks ago they were kind enough to say they could learn a thing or two from us. Maybe that's almost as good!"

Above Ex-GWR 5205 class 2-8-0T No.5224 pilots ex-LMS 4F class 0-6-0 No.4422 over Brooksbottom viaduct on 29th December 1992.

A Classic Light Railway

KENT & EAST SUSSEX RAILWAY
Tenterden - Northiam

The Rother valley, near the western border of Kent, has few communities of any great size. The largest, perhaps, is Tenterden, which in 1911 had a population of 3,376, and was a place of some importance. This it had acquired, long before, as one of the Cinque Ports, and the Harbourmaster of Rye used to live at Smallhythe Place, a little to the south. Things are different today, for the visitor will look in vain for the sea, which now lies ten miles away from the High Street.

The other places the line served were small, so that here, obviously, we have no city railway beset with commuters and rush-hours. The K&ESR has been a part of the landscape for 90 or so years, and the all-pervading atmosphere is one of rural peace, broken only when a steam engine blasts its way up the steep (for a railway) 1 in 50 gradient towards Tenterden station.

Why, should anyone want to build a railway here in the first place? It's a good question, and one which is not easy to answer. Yet the urge must have been very strong because between the 1840s and 1896 there were no fewer than eight schemes for a line to serve Tenterden. The first seven proposals failed but the eighth (the 1896 plan) took advantage of a recently-passed Light Railway Act. It was for a line from Robertsbridge, thirteen and a half miles away in East Sussex, and it was called the Rother Valley Railway.

The Company took some time to acquire its land, but in 1897 the firm of Godfrey & Siddelow was sub-contracted to build the line. The Engineer was a gentleman called Colonel Holman F Stephens, and trains began running from Robertsbridge as far as the station now called Rolvenden in 1900: Tenterden Town was not actually reached until 1903. Two years later it became a

Left Ex-LBSCR A1X class 0-6-0T No.32678 blasts its way up the 1 in 50 Tenterden bank with a mixed train, 12th November 1993.

Kent & East Sussex Railway

Tenterden Town Station, Tenterden,
Kent, TN30 6HE.
Tel. 01580 765155

Route	Tenterden-Northiam (7 miles)
Gauge	Standard
Open	Suns, Feb/Mar/Nov; w/e,b/h, Apr/ May/Oct; daily, Jun-Sep.

Authority was given to build a line between Robertsbridge and Tenterden in 1896, and construction of the Rother Valley Railway, as it was then called, began the following year. The first trains ran in 1900, but only as far as the present Rolvenden station - Tenterden was reached three years later, and an extension was built to the main line at Headcorn in 1905. At this point the Railway's name was changed to the one at the head of this section, and it led a fairly hand-to-mouth existence until BR closed it in 1961. A Preservation Society had been formed the previous year: there was a long, uphill struggle before a decision was made to open from Tenterden instead of the Robertsbridge end, as had been planned, but the first public service began in 1974. Since then the line has been re-opened in stages, first to Wittersham Road and then, in 1990, to Northiam. Work has now re-started at the Robertsbridge end of the line.

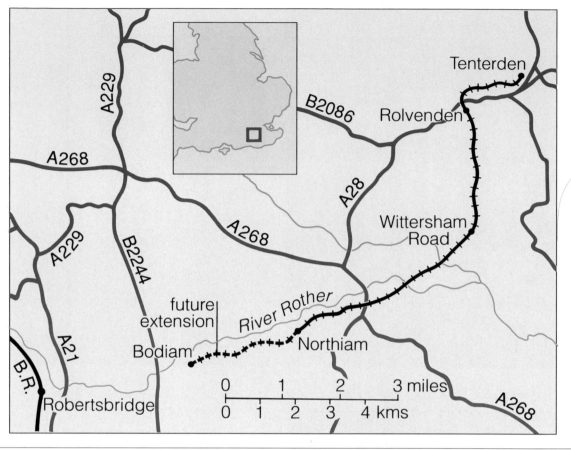

through station when an extension opened to Headcorn, eight miles to the north.

In 1904 the Rother Valley Railway changed its name to the Kent & East Sussex Railway. For 30 years up to 1931 the line was run by Stephens, who attained the rank of Lieutenant-Colonel during the Great War. Born in 1868, he was the only son of F G Stephens, one of the pre-Raphaelite school of painters, but did not follow his father's artistic lead. He studied civil engineering at London University, and then mechanical engineering at the Metropolitan Railway's Neasden Works. He built his first railway at the age of 22, and as time went on he became involved with many minor railways, mostly in Southern England. The Festiniog and Welsh Highland Railways came beneath his umbrella too, and he ran his lines - he came to own sixteen of them - as cheaply as possible, using an incredible variety of second- or third-hand rolling stock.

A kindly man, though a strict disciplinarian, he chose at the 1923 Grouping not to merge his concerns with the Big Four: for this we should thank him, since there would otherwise, probably, have been nothing of the Kent & East Sussex Railway for today's volunteers to restore. He acted as an Inspector for the Board of Trade for a while, but became disenchanted and is on record as saying to a friend in 1927: "The Ministry of Transport are a load of twisters, but I will twist them yet!" In later life a series of strokes deprived him of the power of speech, but he was probably eloquent enough using sign language. He died at Dover, on 23rd October 1931, after which his lifelong assistant, William Austen, ran his concerns. Like Stephens, Austen's name is now carried by one of the

Far right Ex-LBSCR A1X class 0-6-0T No.32650 nears Wittersham Road with a mixed freight from Northiam on 1st May 1993.

Above *Ex-SR USA class 0-6-0T No.DS238* Wain-wright *runs round its train at Northiam on 30th July 1994.*

restored K&ESR engines. Though the East Sussex line had its problems it became Stephens' favourite, and it is fitting that he and his 16-railway empire should be remembered in a museum just a few yards from Tenterden station. The Colonel Stephens Society was formed in 1985.

As with most railways, great optimism was shown for the line's potential, but in fact profits were never good. Indeed, from 1926 losses increased alarmingly. Various ways of economising were tried, but, as in so many things, cutting down on maintenance for instance, while perhaps helpful in the short term, is not a lasting solution. Recycled stock may be cheap at first cost, but it wears out more quickly than new, and since the railway was, in any case, hardly making money there was none available for renewals. Engines, carriages and trucks became more and more run-down as time went on.

Nationalisation in 1948 saw the K&ESR become part of British Railways, and a regular passenger service survived for only another six years. Track between Tenterden and Headcorn was lifted almost at once, but hop-pickers' specials ran between Robertsbridge and

Tenterden until 1959 and freight trains until June 1961. Just before this - on 13th April that year in fact - a society was formed to preserve the line.

Things were not easy. As an early edition of the K&ESR Guidebook says:-

"Little did the founders realise that they had a thirteen year struggle before the first trains were to run."

The application for the British Railways Board to sell the line for £36,000 to the new Rother Valley Railway Company was turned down by the Minister of Transport, Mrs (as she then was) Barbara Castle, a ruling which the Courts overturned on Appeal. This was in 1970. Nothing daunted however, the Society ran its first train on 3rd February 1974, over two miles between Tenterden station and a point south of Rolvenden. Early hopes of having the line open to Bodiam in two years were quickly dashed, but by 1976 services were running as far as the Newmill Channel, about a mile and a half beyond Rolvenden. The bridge at this point had to be rebuilt, and this was not easy, for the foundations stand on 30 feet of unstable alluvium and 60 feet of peat, which is undermined by two geological faults. On the day the bridge was to be lifted into place heavy rain covered the abutments with a foot of water. The 'lift' went on however, and trains were running to the site of Wittersham Road in the following March. The station itself was opened on 16th June 1978. There followed a period of consolidation. Trains were running as far as the 5-mile post, just short of Hexden Channel, in 1984, and a major push in 1990 finally achieved a railhead at Northiam.

For most people, Tenterden Station is where a journey begins. On the right of the train (assuming that you are facing forward) the signalbox dates from 1850, and was transferred from Chilham, near Canterbury, in 1973. All train movements in and out of both Tenterden and Rolvenden are governed by semaphore signals. When the signal beyond the level crossing shows that the line is clear for us, our train puffs purposefully across the lane, and at once plunges down the 1 in 50 of Tenterden bank.

The Act under which the railway was built was intended to make life easier for railway companies by not insisting on heavy earthworks, and the result on this and many other lines was some quite stiff gradients. Though banks as steep as 1 in 50 are not unknown on the 'big' railways, light railways (so called because they

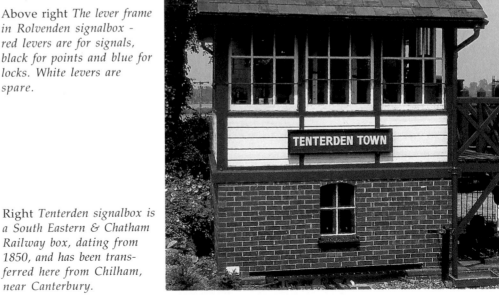

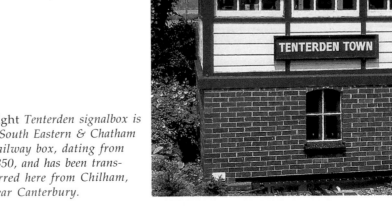

Above left *The Tyers tablet machine in Rolvenden signalbox. Correct usage of such machines could ensure an accident-free railway service.*

Above right *The lever frame in Rolvenden signalbox - red levers are for signals, black for points and blue for locks. White levers are spare.*

Right *Tenterden signalbox is a South Eastern & Chatham Railway box, dating from 1850, and has been transferred here from Chilham, near Canterbury.*

are laid on lightly built earthworks with light materials) made use of the Act as they were meant to, and simply followed the ups and downs of the land. The result usually resembled a switchback, and sharp curves and level crossings were by no means avoided either.

The line's highest embankment, all 25 feet of it, is crossed as the line winds off its spur, and beyond is a cutting where the track level is now some three feet higher than it used to be. A geological fault lies beneath it, and from the carriage window traces of land movement are clear. Newmill Channel is crossed for the first time, and hereabouts one of only two hop-gardens now visible from the line lies away to the right. Time was when hop-pickers in their thousands arrived on special trains during the season. They came to Kent for an annual working 'holiday', and the railway did good business. Nowadays most of the hop-gardens are gone, though the conical roofs of the oast houses, once used for drying the crop,

are still seen as parts of newly-converted desirable residences.

Our train is travelling downhill, but this doesn't, of course, mean that the driver can simply let it roll. There are three more level crossings before Rolvenden is reached, the third being across the busy A28, and I for one would rather not imagine the consternation on both road and footplate at the prospect of a heavily-laden passenger train approaching, at high speed, closed gates across a main road. A point not often remembered by most people is that trains these days are normally far more heavily loaded than any Colonel Stephens saw - the only exceptions in his day, perhaps, would have been the hop-pickers' specials.

If you stand at the level crossing at Rolvenden and look back along the line towards Tenterden, you will see that beyond the curve the line begins to rise steeply. Some years ago a speed restriction was introduced, just where engines climbing the hill would have found a dash at the slope extremely handy. Rabbits were to blame, since for reasons best known only to themselves, the creatures found the ash-based embankment much to their liking. Perhaps the ash was still warm. Anyhow, they colonised it as only rabbits can, and undermined it so much that a speed limit of 10mph was necessary, soon reduced even further to 5mph. Eventually things reached such a state that between February and May 1993 the line was closed, and 500 yards of the embankment were completely dug out and renewed. It cost a small matter of £70,000.

"And has it done the trick?" I asked several people.

"We're hoping so," I was told. "It's early days yet, so we shall have to wait a while and see."

I hope they are right, but the Kent & East Sussex Railway may not have finished with rabbits yet.

Rolvenden station has a single platform, on the left of the line, and behind it is the engine workshop built by the preservation society during the 1970s. The old works was here too, but opposite the platform, on a site now occupied by a timber yard. The original station was completely razed when the line was closed, but the Society rebuilt it as close to the original pattern as it could.

No fewer than six engines were in action during my

Left A perfect reflection. 0-6-0T No.32650 pauses on the Rother bridge with a mixed goods while heading back towards Tenterden on 1st May 1993.

1993 visit - *Holman F Stephens*, painted brown and named after the manager of the line whom we have already met, and *Linda*, a sister-engine resplendent in dark green. Both are 0-6-0 saddle-tank engines and were built by Hunslet, of Leeds, in 1952, having Works Numbers only ten digits apart. When *Linda* arrived in 1977 from the National Coal Board at Maesteg in South Wales she needed a complete overhaul. It was some while in coming and cost £15,000 but on 23rd August 1988 the actor Donald Sinden officially declared her back in traffic. She now has another guise on the Mid-Hants Railway.

Holman F Stephens once worked for the War Department, and, after initial storage and running in at Longmoor, moved to Bicester in 1956, where it was given the name *Black Knight*. Then, after five years in store at Long Marston, its final spell of military service was at Shoe-buryness, from 1968 to 1972, when it was bought for use on the K&ESR.

Also on duty were *Charwelton*, a smaller engine, also in brown, and also a six-wheeled saddletank, but very much older, having been built by Manning Wardle in 1917. This engine came to the line from the Parkgate Iron Company, in Northamptonshire, and is privately owned. It was restored by Resco at their works in Woolwich, and returned to traffic on 18th September 1982 after 16 years out of action.

Sutton, a diminutive tank engine of a type built by the London, Brighton & South Coast Railway over a hundred years ago (*Sutton* in fact dates from 1876) and almost universally known as 'Terriers'. The engine's original number was 50, and it was named *Whitechapel*. Under yet another identity (W9, *Fishbourne*) the engine worked on the Isle of Wight for a period until 1936, and then went into Departmental use at Lancing Works until 1953. As No.32650 it worked on the Hayling Island branch until that line's closure in 1963, when it was bought by the London Borough of Sutton. It came on loan to the embryo K&ESR, and in 1981 a 30-year lease was negotiated, involving the use of its present name. It was overhauled during 1981/2 and went straight into service. The K&ES has had a long relationship with locomotives of this type: small, light, with a short wheelbase, they were ideal for lines like this, and it is fitting that the present situation can maintain this.

No.1556 is another small tank engine, of a type which Col.Stephens used on this line, a Class 'P' tank engine

Above *The interior of SE&CR carriage No.177 as restored at Tenterden, seen on 17th March 1994, just before entering traffic. The view is of the saloon, with the compartment just visible at the far end.*

hessian sacks, called pockets, each holding two hundredweights. In his autobiography, *Drawn From Memory*, E H Shepard (the artist of *Winnie the Pooh* among many others), describes how this job was done in 1887. Hops were tipped into the sack, and a man followed them, lowering himself carefully "...until only the top of his hat could be seen". The man (whose name was Dan) then began to tread, working his way round the sack while more hops were poured in from above: as they were added Dan rose higher and higher.

"The sack shook and vibrated as...it hung from the ceiling like a big cocoon," writes Shepard. "At last it was full, and Dan stepped out and shook himself. He was covered with bits of hop, but he didn't seem to mind. 'Bin doin' it for...twenty-nine year, come next pickin,' [said] Dan."

The pockets, when full, were sewn up with a carpet needle, lifted off by pulley, and made ready for transport. This would inevitably have been the railway at that time. Now, just as inevitably, the hops are transported by road, and, as the late Prof. H P White has remarked, the only time the railway has anything to do with them is in the station buffet.

Bodiam is the railway's next target, though no-one, probably very wisely, is making any predictions about when it will happen. There seem to be two schools of thought at present as to the method of approach. One is to spend a lot of money and get there quickly, and the other is to open short sections towards the destination as completed, running a shuttle service - maybe with a 'Terrier' and a couple of coaches - from Northiam to the current railhead. Both have pros and cons, and perhaps by the time this appears in print a decision will have been taken. Whatever happens, the station building and surroundings at Bodiam have already been smartened up. Platform, trackwork and level crossing need attention, of course, but a start has been made. The wonderful view across the valley towards the village and castle has changed little since Colonel Stephens' day, and one feels it may not be long before rail-borne visitors can enjoy it once more.

And what of the K&ESR beyond Bodiam? Well, they say that every railway has to have a future project up its sleeve, and in the K&ESR's case it is Robertsbridge which beckons. Many problems need to be overcome though. Just beyond Bodiam some of the trackbed has reverted

to farmers, and parts of it have been obliterated. A deviation to the north here is feasible, though this would involve two new bridges across the Rother. The National Rivers Authority has raised no objection, as long as certain provisos are met. Both Bodiam and Robertsbridge, it is felt, would benefit from the return of the railway - Bodiam Castle is already a major tourist attraction, and shopkeepers in Robertsbridge would welcome tourists now that the bypass siphons off much of their passing road trade. A separate railway company has been formed to take charge of this very challenging project.

One of the Kent & East Sussex Railway's 'speciality' fields is the restoration of vintage carriages. Chris Cheney is the man in charge of this side of things at present, and he and Ken Lee were kind enough to spend a morning talking to me and showing me round. There are 20 historic carriages on the line, several of which are still awaiting attention. Already running are an 1887 Great Eastern Railway 1st/3rd composite 6-wheeler which made its return to traffic in 1991, and Metropolitan/District Railway Brake 3rd No.100. Also in traffic at present is an ex-London & North Western director's saloon dating from 1910, another 6-wheeled carriage, with balconies at either end. This vehicle and two others were rescued by the Transport Trust from the Longmoor Military Railway, where they had been used as the officers' 'blue saloon' train. They were moved to the Severn Valley Railway and came on to their present home in July 1985.

The second item of the Longmoor trio returned to work only in 1994 - this was South Eastern & Chatham Railway Family saloon No.177, which was built at Ashford in 1900. It was converted to an invalid saloon in 1908, and in 1927 the Southern Railway renumbered it 7913 and gave it green livery. It was sold to Longmoor in 1936, and now looks superb both outside in maroon paint - the signwriting, incidentally, is another of Chris Cheney's talents - and inside in its upholstery, woodwork and (some) original brass fittings. It also gives an extremely comfortable ride. As presently running there is a long saloon at the western (Robertsbridge) end, with upholstered seats fitted around the walls. At the eastern end is a traditional compartment, and between the two, one to either side of the adjoining corridor, are a washroom and toilet also substantially with their original fittings.

"What," I asked Chris and Ken, "are the problems with restoring old vehicles like this?"

They vary greatly, I was told, though older carriages are often in better condition because better materials were used at the start. Standing nearby, for instance, was a Maunsell carriage dating only from 1930. The soft pitch-pine which had been originally used is not now good, and in such conditions it is often better to take out everything and start from scratch than to try to patch up the bad bits. The 'bad bits' can, of course, occur anywhere, but are often at the ends.

So what next? There is a 'birdcage' - a nickname for a carriage with a guards' lookout projecting above the roof - awaiting attention, and a London & South Western luggage/brake van of 1897.

"Considering its age," remarked Ken, "we're told its in remarkably good condition".

All however, need skilled attention, and that, as well as the perennial cash problem, is the main restriction.

"It's difficult," said Chris. "We can't afford to turn away volunteers, but if you get 22 of them in the carriage shed as we do some weekends, the unskilled jobs they can do run out very quickly. Then there is a wait while the skilled work catches up, and this must be frustrating for lots of blokes who turn up and find there is nothing they can usefully do."

One very useful innovation recently has been opening the carriage shed to visitors, and it has already paid dividends in a tutor from a college at Woolwich. Following a private visit he has now brought parties of students down to carry out paintwork and other jobs as part of their course. And, of course, these youngsters are the next generation of railway preservationists; they should be encouraged in whatever way they can.

In 1948 a note published in the *Railway Observer*, the journal of the Railway Correspondence & Travel Society, read:-

"The majority of the rolling stock of the KESR at Headcorn is being ruthlessly smashed to pieces and burnt...On 17th June the board outside the General offices [at Tenterden] ...was pulled down, and the offices appear to be in the course of vacation, thus writing *finis* to another part of light railway history."

Forty-five years on, and thanks to the preservation society, we know that it was not so.

Right A1X class 0-6-0T No. 32678 as it powers up Tenterden bank against the setting sun on 12th November 1993.

Over the Alps
MID-HANTS RAILWAY
Alresford - Alton

"Crises bring out the best of us here", remarked James Freeman with a grin. "Not that we try to make a habit of it, you understand, but we've got one now, as it happens, so you can see for yourself".

I did.

As James summed up: "We've 108 meals to cook and nothing respectable to do it in!"

The problem was that one of the two kitchen cars on the line was out of use, and a substitute had had to be arranged at short notice, since there were two evening dining trains due to run on the following day. The substitute vehicle had been lying out of use, and needed extensive cleaning. All gas fittings and drainage systems required checking, and a part of the deal was that the red InterCity stripe along the side must be painted out.

I donned overalls and was issued with a brush and a tin of paint. At times like this you realise just how long a Mark 1 carriage is! After lunch I was joined by a member of the Traffic Staff and later the then General Manager, now Chief Executive, Margaret Parker came and wielded a paintbrush too. By the time we finished, the work was almost complete, and when I returned to Alresford next morning the carriage had gone, already marshalled into the dining set.

Many people fondly imagine that once you have acquired your line and a few engines and carriages, running a preserved railway becomes simply a matter of sitting back and counting the ticket money. Anyone who, having read that last sentence, still thinks so should go to the Mid-Hants Railway and talk to a few of the members.

The Alton, Alresford & Winchester Railway was incorporated on 28th June 1861 to extend the Alton branch of the London & South Western Railway for 7 miles to Winchester. In 1865 it changed its name to the Mid-Hants

Left The National Collection's ex-LSWR T9 class 4-4-0 No.30120 pilots ex-SR West Country class 4-6-2 No.34105 Swanage towards Alresford on 4th April 1989.

Mid-Hants Railway

The Railway Station, Alresford, Hants, SO24 9JG.
Tel. 01962 733810/734866(tt)

Route   Alresford - Alton (10 miles)
Gauge   Standard
Open   Please telephone talking timetable to
         confirm details.

The railway between Alton and Winchester came into being in 1861, and was to become a vital link with the Naval Dockyard at Portsmouth. Just before opening, in 1865, the Company changed its name to the Mid-Hants (Alton) Railway, becoming known in due course as the Watercress Line, (a name which it has now adopted as its marketing title) by virtue of the amount of the local product once regularly carried to London. During both World Wars the line was a vital link between Aldershot and Portsmouth, and was often used as a diversionary route for main line services. British Railways finally closed it in 1973, but a Society had been formed to preserve the line shortly before that, starting its service in 1977. Small engines are not so useful on this railway, which has steep climbs on either side of Medstead & Four Marks, roughly the mid-point. A round-trip, in comfortable ex-BR stock, will take around 1 hour 40 minutes, through attractive scenery and well-kept stations. There is a connection at Alton, via the footbridge, with the South Western trains on the 'big' railway system.

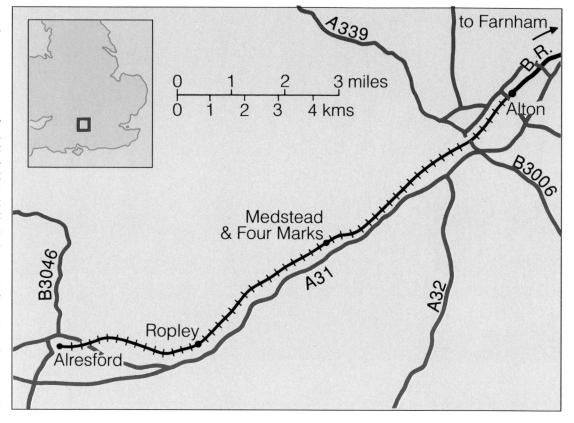

Far right *Ex-LMS Jubilee class 4-6-0 No.5593* Kolhapur *between Alresford and Ropley on 5th February 1994.*

(Alton) Railway, opening to traffic that October. Fifteen years later the L&SWR leased it for 999 years (what optimism) and in 1884 bought it outright. Until its closure by BR it had been often used as a diversionary route, and proved valuable in this role during both World Wars, being a more direct line from Aldershot to the ports.

First steps towards railway preservation in this corner of Hampshire were made in 1972, before the line between Alton and Winchester was closed on 4th February 1973. Negotiations between the newly-formed Winchester & Alton Railway Company supported by the Mid-Hants Railway Preservation Society, and British Rail, resulted in a share issue in May 1975, which attempted to raise £800,000. After six weeks, during which £100,000 had been achieved, this idea was abandoned and a more modest scheme was adopted, to run steam only between Alton

and Alresford - the original had envisaged a daily service using diesel multiple units between Alton and Winchester, Springvale Junction, two miles from the city.

The revised project required only £75,000 by way of funding. Some of the already-raised £100,000 was returned and, and the trackbed almost into Alton's BR station was purchased. Phase 1 of the scheme was to re-open the line between Alresford and Ropley, the track of which was still in situ. That between Ropley and Alton was recovered by BR soon after the first stock had been delivered to the preservationists in March 1976. Hard work through the long hot summer of 1976 was rewarded with a Light Railway Order, and a service began on 30th April 1977.

The first train was hauled by No.31874, a Class N 2-6-0 of a type originating on the South Eastern & Chatham Railway in 1917, and designed by Richard Maunsell. This

Above Ex-SR West Country class 4-6-2 No.34105 Swanage and ex-BR Standard 4MT 4-6-0 No.73080 Merlin (really No.73096) await duty on 3rd July 1994, with ex-SR Merchant Navy class 4-6-2 No.35005 Canadian Pacific (visiting from the Great Central Railway) in the background.

particular example was built at Ashford (the components had been made at Woolwich Arsenal) for the Southern Railway in 1925, serving both in Kent and later in the West Country. Its move in March 1974 from Woodham's scrapyard in Barry was sponsored by a shipping company, Aznar Line, after which it was later named. Restoration went well, and it was hoped to steam the engine in 1975 - alas, the first steaming was a year late, and took place on 4th October 1976. By the end of 1993 the engine was awaiting a heavy overhaul, but, as we shall see, fate was to play a hand in getting her back on the rails rather sooner than expected

An engine shed and workshop was completed at Ropley in 1980, and more locomotives began to arrive. In that year also the MHR paid off its £32,000 loan to BR, and, for £23,000, BR re-arranged its layout at Alton to accommodate MHR trains at the south-eastern face of its island platform. Medstead & Four Marks station, badly vandalised, was taken in hand and restored, and four miles of track between there and Ropley were relaid

between May 1982 and January 1983, totally by volunteers. The plan had been to lay 3.5 miles of track in 13 weeks, but things went adrift, for not only did the laying take longer than anticipated, but the Inspector, during his visit on 24th March 1983, took exception to some of the work as well. By the time his objections had been met - alignments, interlocking, platform surfaces and facings - the first train into Medstead & Four Marks eventually ran on 28th May 1983.

Relaying from Alton to Medstead took from March 1984 to February 1985, much of the work being done in appalling weather. The original hope had been to run the first train at Easter 1983, but the final panel was not actually laid until 12th April 1985, and the first Mid-Hants train to enter Alton - hauled, as ever, by No.31874 - ran on 25th May that year.

Such are the bare bones of what was in truth a mammoth effort. But it took its toll. Heavy borrowing had taken place in order to finance the project, and the creditors needed their money back: the fact that, just about this time, interest rates reached their highest point for years was not, to put it mildly, very helpful. Rumours of bankruptcy began to circulate, and a report that a Receiver had been appointed was stoutly denied by the railway. When however one of the concerns which had promised funding withdrew at the last moment it really was touch and go.

"This was our big crisis," James Freeman told me. "The Bank was threatening to pull the plug and refuse to cash our cheques, but the members dipped into their coffers. Twenty-two of them came up with £55,000 between them in just ten days, and we were able to go round to the Bank saying 'Look what we've got'. Without question, those members saved the railway."

"With hindsight," Ian Dean, the then Managing Director was reported as saying, "the decision to go for the loans was not the right one. It is far easier to raise money for projects than for an overdraft."

In 1988, in an attempt, as it was said, 'to put the MHR back on its feet', an individual takeover bid was made. It was firmly resisted by the Board, and successfully beaten off, but it left a nasty taste, and a sense that the railway really was in deep trouble. Various fund-raising ploys were tried - a Steam-Aid appeal raised £40,000 in nine months during 1992, but this had little effect on the debt, and measures were taken to cut costs. This helped. By February 1994 there had been an upturn in passenger traffic too, and around half of the debt had been paid off.

"We've still not got enough money for everything we want to do," says James, " but then, what railway has?"

Neither was money the only problem. During 1985 the steam service between Medstead and Alton was suspended while pads between the chairs and the sleepers were renewed. Steam engines re-started in traffic on this section on 2nd August 1985. But one cannot escape the conclusion that it was all done much too fast, and if the moral is heeded elsewhere, then perhaps the Mid-Hants traumas have not been in vain.

Let it not be thought, however, that all was wailing and gnashing of teeth down in Hampshire. Far from it, for the will to succeed was intense. Through it all the work has gone on, and the locomotive department has won itself an enviable reputation. A seemingly unending stream of

Right *Ex-GWR Castle class 4-6-0 No.7029* Clun Castle, *a visitor from Tyseley, seen between Medstead and Alton in July 1994.*

quality 'resurrection' jobs comes from Ropley shed: what about some of the others?

No.34016 *Bodmin* arrived in Hampshire in late 1976, amidst hopes that its restoration could be completed by 1979. *Bodmin*, designed by Oliver Bulleid, was built at Brighton in 1945, running first from Exmouth Junction, moving to Kent, and being withdrawn from Eastleigh shed in 1964 after 811,674 miles of service. It remained at Eastleigh as a test-bed for safety valves, but then went to Barry, from where it was rescued in 1972. Some work was done at Quainton Road, the home of the Buckinghamshire Railway Centre, before its arrival at Ropley in November 1976. After time beneath a polythene cocoon - the engine shed was not completed until 1980 - a satisfactory steam test was held early in 1979. Finally, after 30,000 man-hours of work, *Bodmin* re-entered traffic on 8th September 1979, earning a special mention in the annual awards made by the Association of Railway Preservation Societies. The engine had an overhaul during 1985, and, despite a substantial cash-offer for it in 1990, remains on the Mid-Hants, after a further overhaul to main line standards.

The ex-Southern Railway class U 2-6-0 No.31806 is, like No.31874, unique. It was originally built as a 2-6-4 tank engine and carried the name *River Torridge*, but after a series of accidents to members of the class, the tank engines were rebuilt as 2-6-0 tender engines, this one in June 1928. It can claim to be a Hampshire engine, having been based at Basingstoke for several years, but was withdrawn by BR in January 1964, and some time later bought from Barry scrapyard by two MHR directors, reaching Ropley in October 1976. It was hoped to re-steam the engine in 1980: it passed its first steam test on 21st April 1981 and re-entered traffic three days later, having had 20,000 man-hours spent on it. It hauled the first train into Medstead, on 28th May 1983.

There are no fewer than six Bulleid Pacifics on the Mid-Hants at present, but the only other in working order however is No.34105, *Swanage*, a member of the same Class as *Bodmin*, but an unrebuilt example. This locomotive was completed at Brighton Works in March 1950, and spent most of its working life at Bournemouth - it hauled the inaugural 'Royal Wessex' express from Weymouth to Waterloo in May 1951. After withdrawal in

Left Ex-LSWR S15 class 4-6-0 No.30506 between Medstead and Alton, also on 3rd July 1994.

October 1964 it went first to Barry, came to Ropley in March 14 years later and into service, fully restored, in August 1987.

Another pre-Grouping engine on the strength is No.30506, a 4-6-0 tender locomotive designed by Robert Urie for the London & South Western Railway, and built at Eastleigh in 1920. The S15 Class was designed for main line goods working, and No.506 (as it then was) spent much of its time travelling between Feltham yard and a large variety of places. In August 1949 the engine was renumbered No.30506 by BR, and it was withdrawn in January 1964, moving to Barry in June. It was bought by the Urie S15 Preservation Group (later the Urie Locomotive Society) in 1973, reached Ropley three years later, and was back in traffic by July 1987.

No.76017 was built at Horwich, near Manchester, in 1953 as one of the BR Standard Class 4 2-6-0s, and worked throughout its life on the Southern Region, mostly out of Eastleigh. It entered traffic on the Mid-Hants in May 1984. Slightly larger is No.73096 is a Standard Class 5 4-6-0, now named *Merlin*, and carrying the number 73080. This engine was completed at Derby in December 1955, and allocated to the Midland Region. It went to Barry after withdrawal in November 1967. The biggest engine on the line is an American 2-8-0, No.701, also the only foreign-built loco. It served in Italy during the War, and then went to Greece, returning with 2-10-0 No.601, now on the North Yorkshire Moors Railway. No.701 re-entered service in 1990, named *Franklin D Roosevelt*.

As will by now have become obvious, the Mid-Hants has little use for small engines - they simply cannot get up the hill to Medstead, at least not with any sort of a useful load. This too presents its own problems, and the fact that much of the line is in cutting, and overhung by trees, does

Below Ex-BR Standard 4MT 4-6-0 No.73080 Merlin *(73096) seen between Medstead and Alton on 3rd February 1994.*

During those ten days incoming calls to the information office at Alresford were monitored at an average of over 400 a day. Both engines were based at Ropley for the event, and station staff were kept at full stretch with a shuttle service in each direction at half-hourly intervals, *Thomas* taking the easier run to Alresford, and *James* coping manfully with the bank up to Medstead. In 1995 No.31874 returned to BR guise, and No.31625 took its place as *James*.

Great fun, of course, but there is a much more serious side to it all - don't forget that the youngsters enjoying *Thomas* today, may be helping to run the railway within the next 25 years. The future of the railway - and not just this one - is in their hands. We would be irresponsible not to encourage it. After all, if just one per cent of the 29,000 visitors to that *Thomas* event came back as volunteers, and all the present workforce withdrew, the railway would have more working volunteers than it does now!

To its great credit the Mid-Hants has actually done something about looking to the future of the Railway. The idea was floated at a volunteers' meeting in November 1992, when the name 'Watercress Rangers' was also coined. Management liked the idea, and the general response was encouraging, though a few diehards set themselves against it. Two people now co-ordinate the Rangers - John Purver and Rosie Jacob, whom I met firing David Shepherd's No.92203 *Black Prince* on a trip from Alton to Alresford and working like a trojan to keep steam in the engine.

"Many people were either reluctant to accept us or just downright anti," she told me. "But we worked with the people we knew were for us, and the word spread that we weren't just a bunch of delinquent cowboys, but conscientious young people who wanted to be a part of the Railway's future. Slowly we have been joining in activities which would have been unheard of a year ago. First the building group, then the lineside people, and then the locomotive group. Finally we made it to the 'Watercress Belle'."

During 1994 the 'Belle' was short of staff, and senior Rangers were invited to help.

"The Rangers," Rosie went on, "responded by turning up looking super in their black and whites, and working their socks off. The 'Belle' manager was wooed and won, and sang the Rangers' praises all over the Railway. We were made!"

Since then the Watercress Rangers have gone from strength to strength, and if Rosie's commitment and inspiration is typical of the sort of encouragement that they are getting, have no fears for the future of the Mid-Hants Railway.

Left *The point where steam equals motion as the piston (left) meets the connecting rod (right) at the crosshead (centre) - the engine is BR Standard 4MT No.73096 on 4th April 1994.*

Right *Ropley panorama – ex-GWR Castle class 4-6-0 No.7029* Clun Castle *in the foreground, with* Franklin D Roosevelt, *'Thomas' and 'James' behind on 3rd July 1994.*

Deep Into Devon

SOUTH DEVON RAILWAY
Buckfastleigh - Totnes

The line now known as the South Devon Railway began its preserved life as the Dart Valley Railway in 1969, but not in the form to which it was originally laid. That story goes back to 1864, when the Buckfast-leigh, Totnes & South Devon Railway was incorporated as a broad gauge (seven feet and a quarter inch) branch line from the South Devon Railway at Totnes to Ashburton via Buckfastleigh. The first sod was cut at Buckfastleigh on 3rd August 1865, and though there is some evidence that the line was complete to that town by 1868, it did not open until 1st May 1872, when it ran right through to Ashburton. It survived for only 20 years as a broad gauge line, before it was converted to standard gauge in May 1892.

Curiously, although it was the Great Western Railway which had carried out the conversion, and had, in fact, taken over the South Devon Railway in 1878, it did not absorb the branch company until 1897. Wool traffic to Buckfastleigh was heavy, and there was much agricultural traffic, market days at Ashburton being particular busy. In later years however passenger returns were not so good, for the road journey to Ashburton from Newton Abbot could be covered in about two hours less than by rail via Totnes. British Railways closed the passenger service on 3rd November 1958 and withdrew the goods service on 10th September 1962.

First suggestions that the line might be re-opened appeared in the Western Morning News a little more than a fortnight later, on 29th September. Early preservation projects in South Devon had centred around the Kingsbridge branch from Ivybridge, then known as the 'Primrose Line', a marketing name now adopted by the present Society. The Ashburton branch had, as the newspaper pointed out, advantages as a preserved line in superb scenery and easy access at each end. That assumed, of course, that BR would allow traffic to run

Left *Austerity 0-6-0ST No 68011* Errol Lonsdale *heads a Buckfastleigh train along the riverbank near Dartington on 30th July 1994.*

Above *The driver of ex-GWR 0-6-0PT No.7714 awaits the 'right away' from Totnes, 30th July 1994.*

Far right *Nursery Pool bridge, a short way south of Buckfastleigh, as ex-GWR City class 4-4-0 No. 3440 City of Truro (a member of the National Collection) crosses at head of a Totnes train on 20th July 1992.*

first time that a preserved line had had a direct connection with 'Big Brother'.

It was a brave experiment, whose failure was really no fault of the DVR. The first year showed promise, for 20,000 of the line's visitors began their journey at Totnes. Unfortunately this figure declined, and by 1988 had shrunk to a mere 12,000. Meanwhile the charges made for the privilege of using BR facilities continued unabated. The line's stock had to be maintained at BR running standards in spite of its own 25mph speed limit: insurance cover of £1m specific to this operation was required. There were frequent rolling stock inspections, for which the DVR had to pay, involving a journey by a C&W Inspector from Laira (Plymouth) on each occasion. A BR driver and guard had to be present on each train, though they were actually in charge for only about two minutes of every journey, and time for this was charged at a commercial rate. And in spite of the fact that BR charged a commission of 10 per cent on all ticket sales at Totnes, the DVR had to pay an annual charge for running rights and use of the station. Small wonder that after four years, with traffic from this source dwindling, the link was abandoned as uneconomic.

Then in 1990 came a very great change. The Buckfastleigh branch, having lost money for some years, was taken over by a group of volunteers from 13th April (Good Friday), the first day of the new season. Clearly they met with success, for as from 1st January 1991 the line was taken on 25-year lease - it was originally offered for only five years, but was upgraded on the plea that long-term plans would be stifled by such a short period - by a syndicate led by the South Devon Railway Trust, which includes many long-standing volunteers.

"Our dream," said Richard Elliott, the Company Secretary and General Manager, was quoted as saying at the time, "is to install a passing loop at Staverton, see the line fully signalled with semaphores throughout, and install the... footbridge linking Littlehempston with Totnes town".

It should perhaps be explained that, by this time, the loop at Staverton had been disconnected, and this is how it remains at the time of writing. It serves merely as a stock siding, but during a fortnight in February 1995 an Army unit laid sidings at the Buckfastleigh end of the station. The stock was then moved, allowing the loop to be reinstated. An ex-GWR signalbox from Athelney,

Somerset has already been erected between the Staverton end of the loop and the site of the new sidings. Phil Southan, the signalman on duty at Buckfastleigh that day, showed me a draft signalling plan for the new layout: to my untutored eye it looked complicated but will no doubt become refined over time.

My job for the day was Travelling Ticket Inspector/ Assistant Guard. The Guard, I suspect to the surprise of many people, is the man in charge of the train. He has complete responsibility for its safety, and the driver must keep him informed at all times of what is happening at, as it were, the sharp end. I was put under the wing of Jim Kelly, an ex-BR employee, and very experienced in the ways of the SDR. David Wotton, Membership Secretary of the SDRA, and, like myself, an ex-member of the dreaded Inland Revenue, was also with us for the first trip of the day, and we shared ticket inspection duties until, back at Buckfastleigh, he was hauled off to take over as Stationmaster there.

There had been gloomy faces at the Buckfastleigh, for sunny days are not usually recognised as good for business. Perhaps the breeze was making it too chilly to lie on the beaches though, for surprise was shown at the number of folks turning up for the first train. And when, at the Totnes end we also found a good number of people waiting. joy, as they say, was unconfined. It continued too; I reckon the booking office at Riverside that day did almost as much business as the main terminus.

First impressions, whatever one may hear to the contrary *are* important. My abiding memory of a first visit to another line (which had better remain nameless) is of the filthy carriage we travelled in. It would be unfair to judge on what may have been an isolated incident - who knows, that particular coach might have been included in the train at the last minute as an emergency measure, but many might not realise that and be put off railways completely by the experience. That does none of us in the preservation movement any good.

With tidiness and appearance in mind therefore, my next duty, having moved the tail-lamp to the rear of the train, was to walk the train armed with a dustbin bag, removing old crisp-packets, drink cans, straws and other rubbish. Also, because it was a hot day, and the windows were open, it was necessary to dust away the soot from the engine which had blown in and on to the tables. This occupied most of the turn-round time.

locomotives, but Richard Elliott put this into stark perspective as we toured the shed. He indicated a GWR 2-6-2 tank locomotive. No.5526, under repair.

"That," he observed, "is coming along nicely, but has cost over £100,000 so far, and will probably cost as much again before it runs. On the other hand," he went on, indicating the engine behind us, "*Joseph* cost £18,000 in the Chatterley Whitfield sale and, although really bought as a source of spares, is actually a runner. We now have a collection of five Austerities, and sheer economics force us to use them. After all, if we don't keep things running, the visitors simply will go away. At least we can keep going with the Austerities until the GWR engines are back in steam - which is one of the reasons why I fought to get our lease extended from five years to twenty-five."

A good point, but purists need not despair. A GWR pannier tank No.1369 is expected to be back in traffic in 1995. It will be followed into the works by another pannier tank, No 5786. Plans are also afoot for the line's only

Left Austerity 0-6-0ST *No.68011* Errol Lonsdale *enters Staverton on 30th July 1994.*

Below Old enamel *advertisements add to the charm of Staverton station.*

On the next trip, having the train to myself (ticket inspection-wise) the job took longer, and on the first trip of the afternoon occupied me beyond Staverton on the down journey. Not many, I noticed, made their return trips straight away - most went either into Totnes or, at the upper end, to the Butterfly Centre or the Otter Sanctuary. I was several times asked by passengers about Buckfast Abbey also, and how to reach it - an incontrovertible argument, I believe, for a 'preserved' railway to be not simply a ride, but to have something to offer as a destination. In this regard alone, the bridge at Totnes has to be of benefit to the South Devon.

The final train of the day was more lightly loaded - not altogether surprising, but as Jim pointed out you never know how many have stopped off at one end or the other - and the day's final duty was to sweep out the carriages ready for tomorrow's service. The hottest work of the lot, this, and a shower and a relaxing evening were very welcome.

There was disappointment in several volunteers I spoke to that less emphasis is currently being put on GWR

remaining 1400 Class 0-4-2 tank engine, No.1420 *Bulliver* - we shall be returning to this engine later.

Carriage restoration in the early days was not overlooked by the DVR, one valuable project being the restoration of the Devon Belle observation car, now in service on the Paignton line. Work was done too on a collection of four vintage GWR carriages: though these were recently sold, two were repurchased by a member and never in fact left the railway. Those remaining are a clerestory carriage designed by William Dean, built in 1894 and used in Queen Victoria's Royal Train, and a dynamometer car built in 1902 to a design of G J Churchward (who was, incidentally, born in nearby Stoke Gabriel) for testing the performance of locomotives when hauling trains.

Many years ago I had the privilege of doing a little work on another important carriage, one of eight Ocean Liner saloons which the GWR built as de-luxe vehicles for the Plymouth boat trains. Work on No.9111 *King George*, built in 1931, began in the 70s, but was shelved for lack of facilities. With the opening of the new workshop in 1980 restoration began again, and this superb carriage is now included as First Class accommodation on service trains, and is also available for hire as a dining car. Its sister-coach, No.9116 *Duchess of York* (1932) is now also in service on the Paignton line.

Also among the carriage collection is a pair of auto-trailers of a type developed by the GWR for use on branch lines. In 1902 the GWR introduced its 'railmotors' - a carriage combined with a small steam engine at one end. These were quite effective, though two major drawbacks were soon discovered - they could not pull anything extra, and as soon as either engine or carriage broke down the whole unit went out of use - multiple units today have much the same problems, so it seems we haven't learned much in 90-odd years!

The auto-coach seemed to be the answer. These had end windows and a driver's compartment, and were fitted with a full set of driving controls linked to the engine, so that the driver could operate the train even when the locomotive was pushing it. The fireman remained on the engine to see to the fire and to operate the injectors and the ejector to release the brake. This meant that, though

Right Ex-GWR 57xx class 0-6-0PT No.7752 heads towards Staverton with a Totnes train during the summer of 1993.

Above Vintage carriages *were added to the service train on 30th July 1994 for a wedding reception - see also p106.*

Far right The National Collection's vintage 4-4-0 City of Truro *toured the country in 1992 and here we see it again during its SDR visit, at the north end of Totnes station on 20th June.*

the locomotive was a separate unit, the train could travel in either direction without the engine having to change ends. A large gong attached to the driving end, above the windows, was the means by which drivers warned of the train's approach.

And this is the point when we return to the subject of locomotive No.1420. The class of 74 engines was introduced, to a designed by C B Collett, in August 1932 specifically for auto-train (or 'motor-train' as the GWR preferred to describe it) working. No.1420 was one of the first engines on the preserved DVR, and was built in 1933. It reached Buckfastleigh on 17th October 1965, having been withdrawn from Gloucester in February the previous year.

All locomotives of the Class were fitted for motor-train working, and it is hoped that, once the loop at Staverton is re-connected and the signalling finished, No.1420 and the two auto-coaches can be restored to run a shuttle service between, say, Buckfastleigh and Staverton. This would be a unique operation in preservation over this length of line, and would, it is felt, offer a considerable attraction for the railway. Much work needs to be done, however, in overhauling the engine and restoring the carriages, so it remains both an expensive and a long-term project. Some funds have already been collected, and it is hoped that work can begin soon.

The start of the branch was at Ashburton Junction, a few yards outside Totnes station, though mileage was measured from the centre of that station. The present terminus of the preserved line is at an independent station known variously during its existence as Totnes Riverside, Littlehempston and now, officially, Totnes Littlehempston, after a village lying about a mile away beside the main line. I think the namechange is a pity, for 'Riverside' trips far more easily off my tongue at least, is more attractive and memorable and is far more descriptive of the station's site.

That aside however, the actual station has been properly completed only comparatively recently, and has now assumed much greater importance with the opening of a footbridge across the river Dart to connect it with Totnes. The station building was rescued from Toller Porcorum, near Bridport, Dorset, at the end of 1981 and 'topped out' on its new platform on 18th July 1988. The building, originally constructed in 1905, was made largely

of standard pre-fabricated timber sections, and was therefore comparatively easy to demolish and reconstruct. It has been lovingly rebuilt, even down to the furniture in the booking office, and looks superb. Beside it stands a shed recovered from Bovey Tracey and a canopy from Axbridge. The toilet block has been constructed new in the style of the Toller building, and complements it beautifully. The whole complex is set on a curving island platform - it is hoped that, in time, a second platform road will be laid, with a siding beyond it.

For many years there was no public access to this point other than by train: now, thanks to the footbridge, it can act as a interchange between the branch and BR's station, subject to a 5-minute walk. Planning permission for the bridge was granted as long ago as 1982, but it had been a gleam in the management's eye for some time before that. Originally costed at around £70,000, the price rose steadily over the years, though the bridge did not. By the time work actually started, on 18th May 1993 (with an official completion date of 5th July), the cost was approaching £200,000. Some of this has been covered by grant aid and other contributions, and a Loan Stock issue (still open at the time of writing) was made to fund the rest. The bridge is expected to bring the line an extra 20,000 passengers a year from the Totnes end. At the time of my visit (June 1994), Totnes was originating 20 per cent of the passenger traffic, so the bridge is certainly justifying its expense, at least for the present.

As the branch curves away from the main line the valley narrows. A green slope closes in on the right and steepens, contrasting with the wooded course of the river on the left or south side. This soon becomes the west, for the line curves right-handed beside a water-pumping station, and follows the river towards attractive wooded country. Waterworks Crossing heralds another pumping station, and as we pass the first milepost Dartington Hall lies about a mile away, beyond the river, though foliage screens it from the railway for most of the year.

Entering the woods, the line begins to trend first north and then west in a long curve, the river close at hand the whole time. Beyond the second milepost the woods thin a little, Staverton village comes into view, above the railway on the right, and the line crosses a road at Napper's Crossing, named after a lady who kept it in GWR days and retired in her eighties, so it is said. Staverton Mill stands nearby, between river and railway,

Rails Beside the Forth
BO'NESS & KINNEIL RAILWAY
Bo'ness - Birkhill

My first sight of the railway terminus at Bo'ness is one I shall not easily forget. I had been invited to Scotland during the Spring of 1988 in connection with an event at the Glasgow Garden Festival, and since my host lived in Bo'ness, on the south side of the Firth of Forth about 18 miles from Edinburgh, he had arranged accommodation for me there. My hotel room had a view (he may have arranged this also) from about 150 feet above sea level across the Firth of Forth. In the distance lay the Ochil Hills, blue, green and brown in the evening sunshine, with the firth seemingly at their foot, calm and unruffled, the tide well in. And on the foreshore, almost directly below me, lay Bo'ness station. My host took me down for a closer look later on, but, as I said, I shan't easily forget that first view.

The area has an impeccable railway pedigree - a waggonway served a colliery here in 1754, and in 1840 the Slamannan Railway opened a line from coalfields inland to an interchange point on the Union Canal at Causewayend, near Manuel. An extension was authorised to a harbour at Bo'ness in 1846, and opened five years later. In 1865 the North British Railway acquired the Slamannan company, and six years after that was busy weighing up the pros and cons of spending £180,000 - a vast sum of money in those days - on a splendid new harbour at Bo'ness. What probably tilted the scales in favour of the project was that the NBR's deadly rival, the Caledonian Railway, owned docks at Grangemouth, a mere three miles up the coast.

So the NBR built its harbour, and even if the decision was made for the wrong reason, the new facility proved a fine investment for both railway and town. The Caledonian, presumably, was not best pleased at the new development, but could do little about it: for the sake of making its presence felt it applied for (and got) powers

Left *Ex-CR 439 class 0-4-4T No.419 heads a short train towards Bo'ness in May 1990. Dominating the background is Longannet Power Station, with the Ochil Hills beyond.*

Bo'ness & Kinneil Railway

Bo'ness Station, Union Street, Bo'ness,
West Lothian, EH51 9AQ.
Tel. 01506 822298

Route   Bo'ness - Birkhill (3.5 miles)
Gauge   Standard
Open   w/e, Apr/Oct; b/h, daily, mid July-end
        Aug; special events.

One of the earliest of the Scottish railways, the Slamannan, built to carry coal, was granted powers to extend its line from Causewayend to a harbour "...at Borrowstouness" in 1846, opening it in 1851. The harbour, expanded later by the North British Railway, made a good living for a while, and a passenger service served the town until 1956. A freight line still served the colliery at Kinneil and by the time this closed in 1980 the Scottish Railway Preservation Society was already installed a little further along the foreshore. The present Bo'ness station area, unwanted land until the railway came, was developed from 1979, opening to Kinneil in 1984 and Birkhill, the present outer terminus, in 1989. A collection of locomotives and rolling stock had been accumulating at Falkirk for 22 years before it made a forced move from its BR site to Bo'ness in 1988. Trackbed is owned for a further distance to a link with the main Edinburgh to Glasgow line at Manuel. This section crosses the Avon gorge on a spectacular viaduct, but is not yet open for passengers.

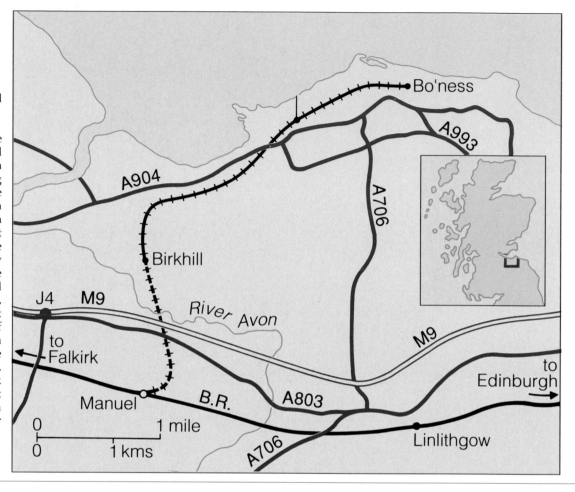

Far right *Ex-NBR J36 class 0-6-0 No.673* Maude *leads a mixed freight across the Avon viaduct on 15th October 1993. Beyond passenger running at present, but perhaps not for much longer.*

to run passenger trains to Bo'ness. It was no more than a gesture, for having used the powers during 1899 only, it ran no more trains. So far as harbours were concerned, however, the CR won on points for Bo'ness, though successful, never surpassed Grangemouth. Bo'ness's best period was during the early years of the 20th century: 2,188 vessels were handled in 1910.

The station which originally served the town lay west of the area occupied by the present station, which was the site of a large siding network used for the transhipment of coal. A passenger service along the old Slamannan line, run by the NBR and, after 1923, by the London & North Eastern Railway, lasted until 1st May 1930, after which passengers for Bo'ness could reach the

town only via a link with the main Edinburgh to Glasgow main line at Manuel. These trains ceased running in 1956, when the line became a freight only branch serving the harbour and Kinneil Colliery. The harbour sidings served as storage for withdrawn locomotives during the early 1960s. Freight traffic along the branch ended in 1965, and 13 years later Bo'ness had nothing left - the 11 miles of sidings which had served the harbour had been lifted, and the area lay derelict.

The Scottish Railway Preservation Society (SRPS) was founded in 1961, and at first based itself at Murrayfield station, Edinburgh. The lack of rail access was a drawback however. Crieff was suggested as an alternative, and Callander, but both proved impracticable, as did the

Above Ex-LNER K4 class
2-6-0 No.3442 The Great
Marquess *(left),* Maude, *and
Hunslet 0-6-0ST stand at the
east end of Bo'ness station.
The Garnqueen signalbox is
on the left, and the
Haymarket train shed in the
background.*

could offer. Since 1964 the Society had leased a large former goods shed at Springfield Park, Falkirk, and the frustrated railway builders proceeded throughout the next 20 years to acquire a remarkable collection of railway locomotives and rolling stock that eventually filled the shed and the yard outside.Meanwhile at Bo'ness, the site of the former railway had been cleared and landscaped, and ownership of the land had now passed to the local authority. If the Society could not afford to buy a complete railway, given open land it could build its own, and Bo'ness was only a mile away from the truncated end of the branch railway at Kinneil Colliery. A lease was negotiated, and by July 1978 planning permission to build a railway had been granted. A first sod was cut at the new Bo'ness station site on 20th May 1979, and by the end of the year buildings were beginning to rise. The plan was to link up with the BR branch which still served Kinneil Colliery, but the first setback was not long in coming: before a single rail had been laid at Bo'ness, BR closed its line.

The price asked for the branch was £113,865, way beyond the Society's reach. BR was willing, however, to split the property into sections, so the SRPS decided to buy 1.75 miles from Kinneil to a point north of the present Birkhill station, plus 142 yards, with check-rails, across the Avon viaduct. This would cost £46,000, and after the grants were taken into account, the Society had to find £15,000. The deal was done, and the work went on.

One of the conditions of the planning permission was that the new station should have a traditional character and harmonise with the old town of Bo'ness. A redundant NBR timber station building, dating from 1887, was located at Wormit, at the southern end of the Tay Bridge. It was bought for £300, and during January 1981 was salvaged by members, dismembered into a kit of parts, and taken south on two lowloaders.

John Burnie, one of the earliest volunteers, was Traffic & Operations Manager at the time of this journey.

"As the lorries crossed the Forth Road Bridge," he remembers, "they overhauled a goods train, also heading south, on the line across the nearby rail bridge: it probably makes our station the only one in existence to have overtaken a train."

The station's reconstruction at Bo'ness illustrates the constant striving after historical accuracy that epitomises whatever the Society does, extending even to the gents'

Longniddry to Haddington branch. An Aviemore scheme had also been abandoned, though some SRPS folks, frustrated at the lack of progress, threw in their lot with the Highlands & Islands Development Board to work on this site. The Strathspey Railway, now growing steadily, was the result.

In 1973 the line from Alloa to Dollar became available when the NCB's mine at Dollar closed. The SRPS set itself to fund-raising for this six-mile stretch of line, but not enough could be collected, and, notwithstanding an interest payment of £8,000 to BR to retain the track, the project, like the others, had to be abandoned. Having walked the Tillicoultry to Dollar section in 1993, I can vouch for the fact that it would have made a wonderful tourist railway - even, as I saw it, in the rain!

As a result of this debacle it was decided to concentrate, for the time being, on the financial stability that railtours toilet, in which many of the fittings, including penny-operated locks, came from Bathgate Upper station, as does the slate urinal.

By May that year sufficient track had been laid to allow a rudimentary passenger service to begin. In fact the first vehicle to run on the line was a bus - railmounted by Lucas Aerospace workers in conjunction with students from the North-East London Polytechnic. The first steam train was hauled by NCB No.24, an Andrew Barclay 0-6-0 tank engine built in 1953. It entered Bo'ness station

on 27 June 1981, proudly bearing the ARPS award for 1980 on its bufferbeam, recognition of the work the Society had done in restoring two other locomotives (*Maude* and *Morayshire* - we shall hear more of them in a moment) to steam. The duties that weekend were shared between No.24, *Clydesmill No.3* and *Sir John King*, a Hawthorn Leslie 0-4-0 saddletank.

"Thankfully an amazing number of members managed to get the day off," says Ann Glen, one-time Publicity Officer. "It was just as well, since much pushing, shoving

Below *Ex-CR 0-4-4T No.419 leaves Birkhill with a Bo'ness train on 22nd April 1990. The hole in the foreground is the site of a proposed signalbox.*

and heaving were required, plus the services of two heavy cranes."

It was a highly successful beginning, the first three months of the rail service accounted for no fewer than 7,000 passengers, who were carried in ex-NBR carriage No.461 and an LNER-design non-corridor brake-composite by Edward Thompson, built at Wishaw in 1951. No.461 dates from 1919, when it was built at Cowlairs: it was converted for inspection duties in 1957, and bought by the Society in 1972.

Despite this wonderful start it was to be another three years before Kinneil was attained. The problem was not of the railway's making. While BR had been in possession, British Petroleum had laid a pipeline from its Grangemouth refinery along the foreshore in connection with its North Sea Forties oilfield. The new railway had to cross this twice, and agreement that it should do so on a concrete raft (at BP's expense) was eventually reached. To minimise the work, the railway would have to deviate from the old line, but before it could do so a programme of land in-fill around Kinneil pit required completion.

Meantime, work went on at Bo'ness. A two-road locomotive shed with a steel and concrete frame went up, clad, in accordance with the planning permission, in red and yellow brick. Window frames from the Glasgow & South Western loco depot at Corkerhill were incorporated. A watertank recovered from Ladybank goods yard was installed. A Caledonian Railway signalbox was acquired from Garnqueen South Junction (near Coatbridge), and a goods shed was built in 1983 to an authentic but unspecified railway design, using re-cycled materials.

Then the Society heard that BR wanted to get rid of an iron trainshed at Edinburgh Haymarket, a listed structure which had been built as part of the Edinburgh & Glasgow Railway's eastern terminus in 1842. Spearheaded by John Burnie, the Edinburgh Trainshed project raised £40,000, and the building was duly moved to Bo'ness and added to the fast-growing complex in 1983. At last, in January 1986 with the 'pipeline' work complete

Left *Privately owned ex-NER J72 class 0-6-0T* Joem *climbs towards High Bridge in September 1993.*

Right *Ex-NBR 0-6-0 No.673* Maude *runs along the foreshore towards Kinneil October 1994.*

and a reverse curve laid across the rafts, a Light Railway Order was granted for the line from Bo'ness to Kinneil - visitors that Easter and since have had a longer run for their money.

Past Kinneil progress was swifter, for now the Society was on the section of track bought from BR. The point where the 'new' line joins the 'old' is just before it reaches the concrete bridge (built in 1991) which carries the A904 across the railway. The line needed substantial attention, of course, before it was fit to carry passenger traffic, but the first train to Birkhill ran on 25th March 1989. It was hauled by ex-Caledonian Railway 0-4-4 tank engine No.419, built to a design of J F McIntosh at St.Rollox in 1907. These engines worked suburban services around Glasgow for many years, and were later the backbone of many a Scottish branch line. It was returned to Caledonian identity on restoration in 1964. Twenty-five years later it bore in front of its funnel a yellow shield emblazoned with the lion rampant of Scotland as it steamed into Birkhill, where an official opening was performed by TV and radio personality Jimmy McGregor on 5th May 1989. As if all this excitement were not enough, the line had a visit from the Prince of Wales three weeks later, during a tour of the area.

A journey along the line begins at Bo'ness beneath the Haymarket trainshed, which is not only impressive in itself on fine days but very welcome on those described in these parts as 'dreich'. Stationmasters were once regarded with almost godlike respect, but even they could never control the weather. Passing the goods shed and the signalbox from Garnqueen, the line passes below a lattice-work footbridge recovered from Murthly, near Dunkeld on the old Highland Railway. This was made in Inverness, and detail work from a similar bridge from Dunbar has since been added.

The dock, now heavily silted up, lies to the right, with the town of Bo'ness to the left. Soon the line curves left, and then, swinging right again, passes the site of the original station - nothing remains visible of either this or Kinneil Colliery. After another right-hand curve we cross the pipeline and are a mile from our starting point, soon to reach Kinneil Halt, for some time the limit of operations along the line. It stands to the south of a landscaped hill of colliery waste bordering the firth, and was opened on 9th August 1986. A passing loop is laid here, but is seldom used these days.

Beyond Kinneil is the point at which the new line links with the branch left by BR after closure. The concrete bridge was built to divert the Bo'ness to Grangemouth road around a notorious traffic hazard called Crawyett Bridge. It could be argued that the railway, when it arrived, caused the problem in the first place, by re-aligning the road in a zigzag through the arch, but in fairness, the road traffic in 1851 was hardly comparable with today's. The problems of latterday juggernauts however were not cured by traffic lights, and collisions between lorries and the bridge became frequent. Finally, as the bridge was in any case reaching the end of its useful life, a decision was taken to re-divert the road. Now the railway has Crawyett Bridge to itself, and trains have a short concrete tunnel to pass through before they begin climbing over the spur away from the River Forth and into the Avon valley. From the railway's point of view,

Below Class K4 No.3442 The Great Marquess *(left) and ex-LNER K1 class 2-6-0 No.2005 in Bo'ness yard as they prepare to work the 'West Highland Railway Centenary' in August 1994.*

Crawyett bridge - the original one, that is - has had careful attention, and is now fit for many more years of service.

As the line passes through the new bridge, the gradient changes from the level of the foreshore and begins to climb at 1 in 95, a gradient it will maintain for most of the remainder of the journey. This stretch is not easy to negotiate, particularly at the time of leaf fall, though by then the traffic of the high season is over. Even in dry weather however, a heavy train and a small engine can present problems. When the foliage on the trees to the right of the line is not too thick, views across the Forth open out briefly. Hereabouts the two-mile mark, as measured from Bo'ness station, is passed, but if you happen to be on the right-hand side of the train you may have noticed mileposts at intervals bearing such figures at 28 and 29. This is because the mileage on the branch was originally calculated from Glasgow High Street station, and the Bo'ness and Kinneil retains these measurements.

Now Grangemouth comes into view, perhaps more impressive than beautiful, after which the line, still climbing at 1 in 95, swings south round the 50 metre contour. In a cutting it passes beneath a high bridge carrying a minor road - here the railway crosses the line of an ancient Roman wall, the Antonine Wall, which once bordered the Forth for some miles. At the end of the curve the line is once more on embankment with open countryside on either side.

The journey is almost over - the three-mile point has been passed, and a vestigial track leads off on the right of the line. This was the site of Birkhill loop, and a branch led to the fireclay mine, of which more in a moment. Cutting begins again, and as the engine reaches another overbridge, the driver will shut off steam to coast into the present terminus at Birkhill. The building here comes from Monifieth, on the line between Dundee and Arbroath: it is yet another former listed structure, and restoration work is in hand. During 1988 it appeared as 'Heart of Scotland' station at the Glasgow Garden Festival.

Another item also at the Festival, though not part of the 'Heart of Scotland' exhibit, was *Lady Victoria III*, an Andrew Barclay 0-6-0 saddletank engine. *Lady Vic*, as she is affectionately known to members, was built in Kilmarnock in 1916, and gained her name from the colliery

Right Ex-CR 0-4-4T No.419 nears Birkhill on 26th March 1989, the second day on which services had run beyond Kinneil.

where she worked. She was delivered to Bo'ness in 1977 and, now in a striking yellow livery, proves very popular with youngsters as an official 'Friend of Thomas the Tank Engine'.

Beyond the station - there wasn't one here originally, and the cutting had to be widened to fit the run-round loop in - lies perhaps the most spectacular part of the line. There is a fall of gradient a little way beyond the station, until suddenly the line runs on to the Avon viaduct, of five stone arches, the railway running some 85 feet above the river. Then, mostly on embankment, the line rises more steeply than ever, leaves the course of the old line, and veers right to run for a short distance beside the present-day Edinburgh-Glasgow main line.

For many the most important locomotive at Bo'ness is *Maude*, No 673, an ex-North British 0-6-0 tender engine of a type designed by Matthew Holmes. This particular engine was built in Glasgow in 1891, and, with others, served overseas during the Great War: on their return several of these were named after Generals or battles of that conflict. The locomotive's final days were spent not far from her present home, working the South Queensferry branch, at the southern end of the Forth Bridge. She was bought by the SRPS on withdrawal at Bathgate in 1966. *Maude* has had a heavy overhaul in recent years, returning to duty on Remembrance Day 1992, when the locomotive was rededicated by Michael Maude, grandson of Lieutenant-General Maude.

No. 246 *Morayshire*, an ex-LNER 4-4-0 tender engine built at Darlington in 1928, and No.24, which we have already met, both belong to the National Museum of Scotland, and both are awaiting mechanical attention at present. North British Railway 4-4-0 *Glen Douglas* has recently been released on a 7-year lease from the Glasgow Museum of Transport, and the SRPS has undertaken to restore this locomotive to working order. It will be an expensive business. *Clydesmill No.3* is a 0-4-0 saddletank engine, built by Andrew Barclay in 1928, for industrial work - it was given to the SRPS in 1970 when it became redundant at the Clydesmill power station of the South

Left Maude *passes Kinneil with a Birkhill-bound train on 24th October 1993.*

Right Maude, *seen from the bridge to the south of Birkhill station, runs round its train in June 1993.*

Above 0-4-4T No.419 passes High Bridge en route to Birkhill in April 1989. Note the Caledonian-style route indicator in front of the chimney.

Far right Ex-LMS Stanier 5MT 4-6-0 No.44871 Sovereign heads a 'North Pole Express' towards Birkhill during the 'Santa Special' weekends, 20th December 1992.

Scotland Electricity Board.

As important as the locomotives is the collection of rolling stock which has been built up from over all over Scotland. Space does not permit a description of each item which may be on view at Bo'ness, but the Society's aim is to have a representative from every aspect of Scottish railway history. This is an incredibly tall order, and possibly not capable of fulfilment, but things are well on the way. At least one carriage from each of the five Scottish railway companies is owned - a royal coach built at Inverurie in 1898 for the GNSR, a Highland carriage of 1909, three Caledonian carriages, three North British carriages and a pair of vehicles from the Glasgow & South Western Railway. There is a large group of more modern vehicles too, many of them unique.

Nor has freight stock been ignored. Freight was the heartblood of the railway in Scotland no less than anywhere else: by 1993 the collection of goods vehicles had reached 80 in number, when there were also 40 locomotives and 40 carriages. It is the ambition of the SRPS to have its collection and site registered as the Scottish Railway Museum, and to this end much requires to be

done. Many of the wagons have already been beautifully restored by a few dedicated volunteers, so a good start has been made.

Fares from a 3.5 mile-long branch cannot possibly pay for all this, you may be thinking, and of course you are right. After all, not only not only do the engines need maintenance but the buildings too, and like every other 'preserved' line, the B&KR needs funds to improve the service it offers to its visitors. So where, then, does the money come from? Funding for some projects has come from local government, and some has come from private sponsors. But do you remember a reference to the 'financial stability' of railtours? A substantial amount of the railway's funding still comes from its railtour business, something which makes it, if not unique, at least different.

Throughout the summer season a group of dedicated volunteers led by James Robertson ensures that the railtour set of BR Mark 1s is clean and mechanically fit to run. Recent legislation has caused extra problems in this area, and one or two train cancellations, but these now appear to have been overcome. Nor does the work stop there. Tickets have to be sold for each train, the train has to be in the right place at the right time, and each one has to be manned, not only with attendants, but the personnel to organise food and cooking for up to three hundred meals per tour. James' wife Elspeth is in charge of the catering, and is, quite simply, indispensable. Elspeth would claim, modestly as always, that teamwork is the vital thing on occasions like this - true, and I don't imagine that anyone would contradict it, but any team has to be led, and Elspeth is a leader *par excellence*.

"The railtour programme means hard work and long hours for most of us," says James, "but there is an enormous reward in bringing a happy and satisfied trainload of passengers home from Mallaig or wherever. And they are satisfied - repeat bookings of up to 60 per cent vouch for that. We can usually manage to make a bit of profit too, which helps the railway."

In 1983, the Bo'ness Heritage Trust was formed with the object of adding to the visitor attractions. In March 1989 the Trust opened to the public the underground workings of the former fireclay mine at Birkhill. This mine yielded a very high-quality fireclay, mined by cutting tunnels laid out in a grid formation, on a site to the south of the river Avon. Having been excavated, the clay was brought up to the processing plant above the mine - higher, even, than

the railway - by way of a bridge across the river and a steep rope-hauled incline. The incline, sad to say, is not in working order, but part of it has been adapted to allow visitors down to the level of the mine, where guides take them through the workings to discover not only how the clay was extracted, but to see fossils and other geological aspects of the mine.

In 1993 the Heritage Trust was superseded by the Bo'ness Development Trust, which has the aim of continuing development of the mine and at the same time of enabling the development of the Scottish Railway Museum at Bo'ness. The Museum will include the present operating railway, extended by 1.5 miles to Manuel, and with much-improved station facilities, as well as new buildings at Bo'ness to permit the story of Scottish railways to be told. It is, however, fundamental to the museum concept that locomotives and rolling stock will not be irrevocably 'cotton-wooled' in the indoor displays. Suitable items will be operated from time to time on the working railway so that they can be enjoyed in authentic surroundings.

Now that the Development Trust is acting as project co-ordinator and fund-raising agency, rapid developments are hoped for. The 1995 season will feature the Scottish Railway Exhibition, an indoor display featuring some of the more remarkable items in the collection, and with an emphasis on explaining the importance and variety of goods traffic. In addition it remains to extend branch passenger traffic beyond Birkhill. Track is in place right up to the main line junction, and though it is used by works trains and the railtour set when required, is not fit for public running at the time of writing, and neither is there any passenger accommodation at Manuel. This will take about £50,000-worth of finance and a good deal of volunteer labour to achieve. 1996, I was told, is technically feasible, but only if the money is found.

Developments at Bo'ness are intended to be extensive, and first on the drawing board is a redeveloped station building intended to provide much-improved public services. Then there is the main indoor display building. For this purpose SRPS have on site the dismantled framework of an industrial building, originally built as the machinery hall at the Glasgow International Exhibition of 1888. Not only could this provide a static display, but it could also function as a heavy repair workshop for locomotives. In addition, a modern motive power depot is

Above *Andrew Barclay 0-4-0ST* Clydesmill No.3 *shunts a demonstration freight at Bo'ness on 27th April 1991.*

Right *Ex-LNER A2 class 4-6-2 No.60532* Blue Peter *winds past Kinneil and along the foreshore in September 1994.*

needed as a home for the extensive diesel locomotive collection, itself an important part of railway history. To enable the conservation of the carriages and wagons, a further workshop is planned, together with a separate paintshop. The Museum is indeed a major project, but given the progress made so far will happen, one suspects, sooner rather than later. "The story of the railways," writes the author of the current Guide Book, "mirrors Scotland's rise in economic importance and prosperity. It needs to be told properly."

John Burnie, who has been assigned the task, admits it is no sinecure.

"We have to make it user-friendly," he said with a grin. "We need to interpret these items in a way that is interesting and easy to understand. A long row of goods wagons is not everyone's idea of a jolly day out, perhaps, but it can be presented without being boring, and we are finding a way."

Back in about 1990 a friend complained to me that he had been to Bo'ness and come away again because "...nothing much seemed to be happening." I suspect that he didn't look further than his car windscreen. Given that the B&K began running only in 1979, it has come a remarkably long way since; I shall be advising my friend to go and have a other look, and this time to make it a longer one.

Coming Back on Line
VALE OF RHEIDOL LIGHT RAILWAY
Aberystwyth - Devil's Bridge

"British Railways," ran a news paragraph in the September 1967 issue of *Railway World* magazine, "is considering selling the Vale of Rheidol to an outside organisation since it is failing to meet its costs of operation... Although increases in passenger traffic have taken place over the past three years the revenue therefrom has not been sufficient to offset the costs of operation."

Privatisation is clearly no new idea, is it?

In my younger days, well before even 1967, I used to think that the valley which this well-known railway followed into the hills was that of the river Ysytwyth, and puzzled why the line was called the Vale of Rheidol Light Railway? In time, and on being directed to a good map, one learned that the river from which the town took its name entered the sea on the southern side, and that the light railway, following a tributary valley belonging to the river Rheidol, was not wrongly titled. What the map could not tell me was just how spectacular a trip along the railway was and, thankfully, still is.

In fact the scenery is but one of several unique properties of the line. It is the youngest line featured in this book - though not by very much, for the Kent & East Sussex beats it in opening date only by two years. It was also, between 1968 and 1988, the only steam operation run by British Railways, and was the first of its running lines to be, as it were, privatised.

The idea of a railway to Devil's Bridge was mooted as long ago as 1861, and the Manchester & Milford Railway was authorised to build it, though not along the present route. Money was always a problem for this Company however, and, for this and various other reasons, nothing happened. After the passing of the Light Railways Act in 1896 a meeting was held in Aberystwyth to consider primarily a line from the station to the harbour, but also a

Left VoR 2-6-2T No.7 Owain Glyndwr pauses at Aberffrwd with a well-filled Devil's Bridge train on 14th August 1994.

Vale of Rheidol Light Railway

The Locomotive Shed, Park Avenue,
Aberystwyth, Dyfed, SY23 1PG.
Tel. 01970 615993 (9th Apr-6th Oct)/625819(Other times)

Route   Aberystwyth - Devil's Bridge
             (11.75 miles)
Gauge   1ft 11¾ in
Open   Varies - please telephone for details.

The company authorised to build this line, the Vale of Rheidol Light Railway, was authorised on 6th August 1897. It was built with an eye to tourists as well as freight, right from the start, but it was the freight which failed first. After being taken over in turn by Cambrian Railways (1913) and the GWR (1922), British Railways ran the line, latterly as its only steam operation, until 1988 when it was sold to the Brecon Mountain Railway Company. Much refurbishment has been done, but in appearance locomotives and stock remain much as they have done for years. The journey takes an hour in each direction along a route of spectacular scenery. The waterfalls at Devil's Bridge are well worth breaking the journey to see, and it is to be hoped that the line is now on the way back to popularity after a period in the doldrums.

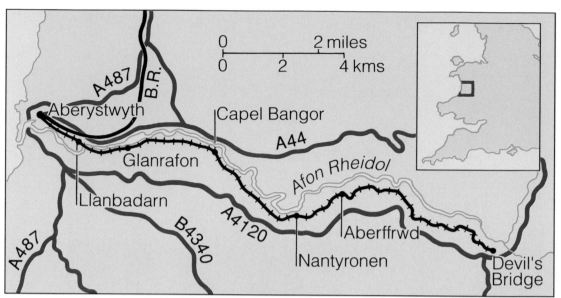

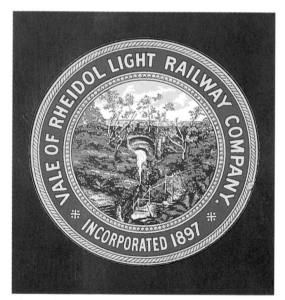

The Railway's crest on the cabsheet of No.7

VoR 2-6-2T No.9 Prince of Wales *at Devils Bridge, 8th September 1991.*

railway south along the coast to Aberayron. The Vale of Rheidol Light Railway Company was authorised in 1897, on 6th August.

The line was to be built in two sections, to a nominal gauge of two feet - in fact it is 1ft 11¾in - though it had powers to widen this to standard gauge if it obtained Board of Trade consent. The Company found capital difficult to find, but a start to the construction was at last made late in 1900, the Engineer being Sir James Szlumper, who had completed the Lynton & Barnstaple Railway, a line with similar engineering problems, two years earlier. Much material and equipment came from the contractor's recently completed job at Blagdon Reservoir, in Somerset, and a locomotive and 15 wagons were bought from the defunct Plynlimon & Hafan Tramway, which served leadmines some miles north-east of Aberystwyth: sometimes known as the Hafan & Talybont Tramway, this ill-fated project had closed in 1900 after a working life of only three years.

Many navvies came to work on the line on completion of the Birmingham Corporation's contract for reservoirs in the Elan Valley, across the hills beyond Devil's Bridge. The trackbed was almost finished by the end of 1901, and the first goods trains ran in August 1902. The line was passed as suitable for passenger traffic in October, and the formal opening took place on 22nd December 1902. Business was good to begin with - passenger journeys were at around 100,000 annually, and goods traffic around 5,000 tons. The freight traffic consisted of lead and iron ores, and sulphur also was exported from Aberystwyth to Belgium and Ireland. The most important mine, the Cwm-Rheidol producing lead ore, was on the north side of the valley, and not, therefore, conveniently sited for the railway. A connection was made by an overhead wire ropeway to a siding at Rhiwfron Halt, but the mine closed during the Great War.

The promoters had clearly had an eye to tourists as well as goods, and it is fortunate that they did. As traffic from the mines began to wane, the line was taken over in 1913 by the Cambrian Railways, but that Company did little to liven things up. Shortfalls in lead traffic were not being made up by other commodities, so perhaps it was fortunate for the new owner that at about this time

Right VoR 2-6-2T No.7 Owain Glyndwr *heads a train away from Devil's Bridge towards Aberystwyth in August 1994.*

Above *VoR 2-6-2T No.7 Owain Glyndwr is about to run round its train at Devil's Bridge, 15th August 1994.*

Far right *VoR 2-6-2T No.7 Owain Glyndwr whistles a warning as it approaches Nantyronen with a down train, in August 1994.*

with selling the line off. This was, of course, long before the present privatisation plan was devised, and, as might have been expected, it aroused a good deal of opposition. Potential preservation plans began to be developed while BR, rather characteristically, denied and confirmed the rumours by turns, until it finally called for tenders on 1st June 1988. A consortium of the line's staff supported by a group of preservationists, was outbid by the Brecon Mountain Railway, which took over the line in 1989. Tony Hills and Peter Rampton had founded the Company, established a custom-built station at Pant, north of Merthyr Tydfil, and constructed 2 miles of 1' 11.75" gauge railway along the trackbed of the old standard gauge line between Brecon and Merthyr.

By now, of course, after some years of neglect, the whole Rheidol concern was very run-down. At once the new owners embarked on a course of refurbishment, admitting at once that changes would not take place overnight, and that it would take some time to take care of all the things they would wish to do.

"We've got to look after our passengers," Tony Hills was reported in *Railway World* as saying in 1991. "We need to build up our passenger figures, and satisfied customers are the best advert. We are talking with the Forestry commission about cutting 'view gaps' in the trees, and we are considering some sort of upgrading in the third-class seating, which are, at present, wooden benches".

One of the first tasks of the new company, obviously, was to put these arrears in order, and an urgent list of priority requirements was drawn up. Track was one of these: it was very poor in some places, and passengers had been complaining of poor riding in the carriages. By 1992 this had been put right, and a ten-year plan for renewals had been drawn up. This allows for replacement of all worn medium-weight rails, and for the section below Aberffrwd to be relayed using heavier (75lb per yard) rail. All are now screwed to the sleepers instead of being spiked as they have been in the past. Level crossings will receive attention too, and consolidation of banking in the upper stretches of the line is also on the programme. Scheduled for attention during the 1989/90 winter was the replacement of the loop at Aberffrwd (pronounced Aberfrood), which had been removed by BR in 1963. The most costly of all was the renewal of the timber trestle bridge across the river Rheidol near Llanbadarn, on the

passenger traffic began to build up. Then came the Great War, after which the Great Western Railway absorbed the Cambrian Railways as part of the arrangements under the 1923 Grouping. The GWR appears to have lacked any great commitment for the line - it meandered on, purely as a tourist attraction, for goods trains ceased running during the mid-20s. New engines and stock were supplied by the GWR during the 1920s and 1930s, and the line closed for the duration of the Second World War.

Then came Nationalisation in 1948. Passenger journey figures rose from 34,000 in 1954 - about the time when I was being puzzled by the line's location - to 96,000 in 1975, but this became a peak. During the long hot summer of 1976 trains were often cancelled because of the fire risk to the Forestry Commission property through which the line runs. Many disappointed prospective passengers did not return, perhaps for this reason, but by 1977 a recession was biting anyway. By 1980 carryings stood at 60,000, and at last a rather more positive effort to publicise the line began.

It seems to have been from around about this time that renewed rumblings began to be made by BR in connection

eastern outskirts of Aberystwyth.

The locomotives, too, have now had overhauls, having been taken to the BMR headquarters near Merthyr Tydfil, for the purpose. Here, in a well-equipped workshop, there are not only perhaps the best narrow-gauge facilities in the country, but the added advantage of a test-track just outside the door, of which good use is made for running-in purposes. And a change of motive power for the visitors to the BMR is probably seen as welcome too. The old BR shed at Aberystwyth now confines itself to light repairs and as covered storage for both engines and stock.

What of the engines? Well, the one acquired from the Plynlimon & Hafan spent most of its working life on the harbour branch, its short wheelbase and lightness making it ideal for that purpose, and the other engines were too heavy anyway. It was withdrawn in 1924 and scrapped. A pair of 2-6-2 side-tank engines was built by Davies & Metcalfe for the opening of the line, and numbered 1 and 2 - the first was named *Edward V11*, and the second *Prince of Wales*. Both were withdrawn for scrapping by the GWR, No.2 in 1924 and No.1 in 1935.

The GWR did, however, build three new engines, and it must be something of a compliment to the original builders that it worked to a very similar design. The new locomotives were numbered 7, 8 and 9, and named *Owain Glyndwr*, *Llewelyn* and *Prince of Wales* respectively. Once the first two were in action the two originals were taken to Swindon. All three engines were converted to oil-burning in 1978/80, in deference to requirements of the Forestry Commission.

Under the line's new owners all three engines have or are being overhauled at Pant. No. 9 *Prince of Wales* went first and had a complete rebuild, using a slightly taller cab. This has, it seems, upset some of the purists, but is much more practical.

"The crews," remarks Neil Thompson, the line's Manager, "can now actually stand up in the thing, which has to be an advantage!" He speaks with feeling, since he had to drive in the old cab on occasion.

Air brakes too are part of the new locomotive design, and all the coaching stock has now been converted also. Locomotive No.7 underwent heavy boiler repairs during the winter of 1991/2, and in 1993 No.8 went to Pant for treatment similar to No.9. It is expected back at

Above Cab interior, VoR 2-6-2T No.9 Prince of Wales at Devils Bridge, 8th September 1991.

Right VoR 2-6-2T No.7 Owain Glyndwr enters the loop at Aberffrwd with an up train on 14th August 1994.

Far right VoR 2-6-2T No.7 Owain Glyndwr seen on its downward journey soon after leaving Devil's Bridge, 15th August 1994.

followed by a further one to the left to avoid having to cross the river at this point. An easier curve to the right brought the line between river and main line, and here an exchange siding was laid between the two railways. The main line had taken rather less than a third of the distance travelled by the narrow gauge line to reach the same spot!

Since the closure of the Carmarthen line in 1965, the Vale of Rheidol line has been diverted to use the Carmarthen bay platform. Entirely sensible, this, because not only does it eliminate those three sharp bends and about half a mile of distance from the route, but also brings the line more conveniently to its customers, some of whom do still come by train. Not as many as Neil would like, but the problems of producing a timetable which will satisfy both parties are horrendous. These days the site of the second station is a supermarket, the site of the first a carpark/bus depot.

The building in which you will buy your ticket for a journey along the line is not original, but it does replicate, as far as has been possible, the structure which the original company used. Then you will pass behind the bufferstops and down a ramp to ground level to board the train, probably of five coaches, including at least one open vehicle and some first-class accommodation.

"We like to give our passengers as much choice as possible," remarked Neil Thompson.

Nowadays the line, on leaving the platform, skirts the old BR engine shed. For years the carriages stood outside until it was realised that there was quite enough space in the shed for all of them plus the engines too! There are sixteen carriages, enough for three five-car sets, though in practice two are usually sufficient at present. These can be strengthened to seven cars if needed, but though the engines could cope with eight - just - seven is the maximum that can be accommodated in the loop at Aberffrwdd. Five-coach trains give a carrying capacity of about 800 passengers (no 'customer' nonsense here) per day, when the four-train timetable is used, during the last week of July and in August. The remainder of the season, on either side of that period, is run with a two-train service.

Beyond the shed the old BR water column still stands, rusting, hoseless and forlorn, and the site of the interchange siding is soon reached though there is now no sign of it. About here you may catch a fleeting glimpse of the three-quarter mile post, though the train has travelled rather less than this. Don't worry, you are not hallucinating

Above VoR 2-6-2T No.7 Owain Glyndwr *sets off from Nantyronen with its Aberystwyth-bound train on 14th August 1994.*

Aberystwyth late in 1995. No.7 will go back for a rebuild towards the end of the 1990s.

Liveries have varied, particularly in recent years, when the 'original' VoR ochre livery has been used, Cambrian black, Brunswick green with lining and a deep crimson - the Brecon Mountain Railway's colours - which certainly looks very handsome on No 9 at present. But at least they are all an improvement, in this writer's opinion anyway, on the BR blue in which the engines appeared for a time, some even sporting large white 'go-fast' arrows! And there may well be more changes. After all, as Tony Hills says, a livery is only a coat of paint.

There have been no fewer than three termini at Aberystwyth. The first stood at right-angles to the main line, about opposite the Carmarthen platform-end, to the south and across a road from it. In 1924 the curve which had led into this station was eased slightly, and the line extended across the road and round a further right-angle to bring it alongside the main-line station. This meant that a train leaving the station went round two square corners, first right, then left, to pass beneath the line to Carmarthen,

- the mileposts still indicate the distance from the second terminus.

The line runs straight and level, heading in a south-easterly direction, and reaching the village of Llanbadarn just over a mile from the start. A trunk road crosses both standard and narrow gauge railways at this point; the BR crossing has barriers, but the VoR one does not, a fact that has caused some contention in recent years.

A few yards beyond the road crossing comes another of a different sort, as the line runs on to the timber trestle bridge across the River Rheidol. This had seven spans and needed considerable attention when the new company took over. Obviously a priority job from the safety point of view, it was entirely rebuilt with six spans and five trestles during the winter of 1991/2, using new piles of greenheart wood, tough and rot-resistant, with stainless steel fixings. The work took three months and cost £140,000.

The 'big' line has climbed and curved away to the north by now, but the narrow gauge still keeps to the river valley. On the left an area of gorse lies between railway and river, with grazing land to the right, backed by tree-lined slopes. Glanrafon station stood at the 2.75-mile mark, just beyond an ungated level crossing. There is no sign of the station now, but the site is marked, on the south side of the line, by a nameboard which also bears the height of the line above sea-level, in this case 31 feet - not much, considering the journey is almost a quarter over! An industrial estate has grown up here - perhaps this may lead to re-instatement of the station.

The climb remains gradual for the next three miles. During this time the line has made its way to the southern side of the valley, passing one or two farms on the way, and reaches Capel Bangor.

We are 4.5 miles from the start now and 75 feet above sea-level. There was a loop (removed in 1963), a station building and a timber carriage shed here once - now only the station building remains, forlorn and, it has to be said, somewhat sad-looking. Capel Bangor, Neil Thompson told me, would be the logical place for a second loop should traffic eventually justify it: there is ample space, and it would split the line into three sections of more or less the same length.

Another crossing, of the lane leading across the valley to the village from which the station gets its name, comes immediately beyond the station, and, for the first time, we sense that the engine is beginning to work harder. The line

is running on a noticeable embankment, the valley side nearer to the south and the river close beneath it to the north. Soon the railway assumes a shelf on the south side of the valley, and gradient posts indicate a climb at 1 in 40. The leaflet issued with my ticket indicated that the steepest slope on the line is actually 1 in 48, but don't be fooled. Neil is of the opinion that most grading on the line is fairly approximate, and that if he had the time and equipment to re-do the survey he would fully expect to find pitches as steep as 1 in 35. The engines are not helped on the banks by the curves, sharp in places, which are necessary to keep the railway clinging to the hillside.

Nantyronen is the next station: the siding that was once here has been lifted, we have climbed to 197 feet and completed slightly over half our up journey. This was a watering point at first, but the facility was moved to Aberffrwd after it was found that the engines were running short of water on the final steep climb to Devil's Bridge. In later BR days the waterstop was moved back here, where it has been retained under BMR control. Despite rumours that it is to be moved back to Aberffrwd now that the loop has been re-installed there, Neil Thompson discounted the possibility.

"It's not necessary," he pointed out, "and it makes a

Above VoR 2-6-2T No.7 Owain Glyndwr waits departure time at Aberystwyth on 15th August 1994. The building on the left is not part of the station - it is a supermarket!

Above *The VoR observation car, seen on departure from Aberffrwd, 14th August 1994.*

Below *The station nameboard at Rheidol Falls.*

point of interest for the passengers, which would be lost if the tank was moved. We have tried to create these points of interest all along the line - the heights above sea-level displayed at each station for instance. Besides, if passengers were to get out at Aberffrwd to photograph both the watering and a crossing, think of the havoc it would play with the timetable!"

The line now winds through woodland, rising slowly higher above the valley floor and proceeding in a series of steps alternating between level and a gradient of 1 in 50. Aberffrwd is a mile beyond Nantyronen and 253 feet above sea level, the railway having so far climbed 239 feet. Aberffrwd station did not open with the line, but a year later, partly at a request from the Urban District Council of the time and partly to provide a watering place for the engines. There was a passing loop (added in 1905), waiting shelter, ground frame, and, of course, the watertanks, for which a hydraulic ram was installed to supply the water. Trains re-passed at Aberffrwd on 9th July 1990, the first time for 27 years.

The replacement of the loop here will mean a greater flexibility in the operation of the railway - without it the only place where trains could pass was at Devil's Bridge, which meant that one train could not set off down the line until the second had arrived at the terminus. This inevitably led to overlong waiting periods between trains, and the 'new' loop will, it is hoped, reduce these considerably. There is, of course, little sense in bringing a train straight back - after all, passengers usually travel to Devil's Bridge because they want to see what is at the other end, the Mynach falls and/or the Devil's Bridge itself. To give them insufficient time to do so would be pointless.

Above the level crossing which lies immediately beyond Aberffrwd station is perhaps the most dramatic part of the journey. Several derelict mines are passed, though the years have shrouded their remains in greenery and it is hard now to pick them out unless you know exactly where to look. Even Cwm-Rheidol, once a very obvious scar across the valley, is less clear than it once was. Some of these mines were briefly worked after initial closure, but their winnings were all taken away by road. Now most of the shafts are flooded.

There were two halts along this stretch, but, were it not for the markers (on the valley side of the line), the passing traveller would be hard put to it to spot the locations now of Rheidol Falls (425 feet) at 9.25 miles and Rhiwfron (542

feet) at 10.75. The trackbed shows a widening at this point, where the siding once was, but the only sign of what might have been anything to do with the cableway to the mine is a short pillar some ten feet high, built of slate, standing to the right of the line - could this have been one of the cable supports? A steep, spectacular-looking and possibly inaccessible series of waterfalls can be seen descending a cleft on the far side of the valley - curiously, I cannot recall having noticed them before, in several visits to the line.

Neil Thompson is very conscious that the scenic beauties of the line are not, at present, shown to their best effect. The talks to the Nature Conservancy Council about view-gaps progress only slowly, and in any case, he says, his men have their work stretched to keep the under-growth between the fences in check. Twelve miles of line means twenty-four miles of verges, all of which needs clearing once a year. With the best will in the world the limited resources at his disposal can't do all this and keep the trains running too! There are six paid full-time employees besides himself, and extra part-time staff are taken on to help out during the summer. "That's how I prefer it," he said.

"Supposing half a dozen lads turned up here tomorrow," I suggested, "and told you they'd work for six weeks for nothing except the pleasure of doing something for the railway."

"If I could afford it I'd pay 'em," he shrugged, "because then I'd be in a position, supposing an emergency requiring ten blokes on, say track, arose, to be able to tell the lads to join the track gang without the risk of them simply melting away muttering that they had only volunteered to cut bushes."

From Rhiwfron it is barely a mile to the terminus. The line winds along its sinuous shelf, until, after an enormous curve where, from the tail of the train one almost feels one could shake hands with the engine driver, the train plunges into a short rock cutting. On emerging there is, on the right, a ledge above line level, where, it is said, stood the accommodation in which the navvies who built the line were housed. Below the line, on the left, are the remains of an old woollen Mill, now almost concealed by trees and overgrowth.

Still working hard, and swinging sharply left again, our engine dives beneath a bridge - now the only overbridge on the line - to draw to a halt at the Devil's Bridge terminus, 639 feet above sea level. In four miles the line has risen 386

feet, which produces an average gradient for the section of 1 in 54.7, though one suspects, along with Neil, that some pitches are considerably steeper than that.

The coaches in which the passengers enjoy their ride these days were supplied new by the GWR in 1923 and 1938, after most of the original stock had been scrapped. Some vehicles are open, but, in recognition of the indisputable fact that it does sometimes rain heavily in Wales, there are closed carriages too. All the open vehicles have glazed ends - after all, this is perhaps the most spectacular train ride in the UK - metal sides with mesh to waist level, and canvas screens for use in wet weather. Seats are reversible, tramway fashion, and each vehicle holds 48 passengers.

Also on the strength is one Vista Car, fully glazed, but with a lower waist on the 'vista' side. It was out of use on the day of my visit - apart from the fact that the weather scarcely warranted it, its windows were mute witness to

the fact that there are vandals even here. Why is it that unattended glass seems to present such a lure to idiots with stones, bricks or iron bars? Perhaps a just retribution, supposing that our strange legal system allowed for any deterrent more effective than a caution, might be to make these mindless louts take out the broken glass with their bare hands.

"When folks ask me to define railway preservation," said Neil Thompson, "I tell them that what they see on the Vale of Rheidol is the closest they'll get to it. Here we have an independent company, with a small paid staff, working a line on the same trackbed and for the same purpose as it was built in 1902. The locomotives and stock, though not the originals, were built for the line, and otherwise the only thing that has changed is that we don't carry freight any more. With the greatest respect to them, very few of the so-called 'preserved lines' can match that, I think."

He has a point, hasn't he?

Above *VoR 2-6-2T No.7 Owain Glyndwr heading a down train, approaches Capel Bangor station on 15th August 1994.*

Launceston Steam Railway

St.Thomas's Road, Launceston,
Cornwall, PL15 8DA.
Tel. 01566 775665
Route   Launceston-New Mills (2 miles)
Gauge   1ft 11⅞in
Open   Easter to October with some seasonal
         variations.

This line is laid along the trackbed of the old London & South Western route to North Cornwall, opened in 1886 and closed 80 years later. The present railway began work in 1983, and from small beginnings has grown steadily. Five steam engines come from quarries in North Wales, though not all are yet working, and the coaches are replicas of various narrow-gauge prototypes. A short extension from New Mills is planned, along with development at the Launceston terminus.

Lavender Line

Isfield Station, Nr Uckfield, East Sussex.
Tel. 0182 575 0515
Route   Within station site (0.75 mile)
Gauge   Standard
Open   Steam on Suns, Bank hols; diesel Sats.

Isfield station was bought by David Milham in 1983 and transformed from wilderness to showplace, with passenger and dining train services. In 1991 Milham decided to sell, and, after some uncertainty, volunteers took over in November the next year. One and a third miles of trackbed are owned, and the rails will be extended as time and cash permit. Two steam engines are on-site, and a 5in gauge miniature steam line at Isfield is also projected, with a relaunching of the dining trains.

Leighton Buzzard Light Railway

Pages Park Station, Billington Road,
Leighton Buzzard, Beds, LU7 8TN.
Tel. 01525 373888
Route   Pages Park-Stonehenge Works
         (2.75 miles)
Gauge   1ft 11½in
Open   Suns, Bank hols end Mar/begin Oct,
         Weds, Thurs in August.

The railway was built to serve sandpits during WW1, but when the pits closed in 1969 the present Society took over the running of the line. The first steam engine Chaloner, came in 1977, and since then much has been improved - facilities at Pages Park, for instance. Rolling stock has been obtained or built, more steam engines have arrived, and the line has been extended to its present terminus. Here a museum is planned to illustrate the Society's historic connections.

Llanberis Lake Railway

Padarn Country Park, Llanberis, Caernarfon,
Gwynedd, LL55 4TY.
Tel. 01286 870549
Route   Gilfach Dhu (Llanberis)-Penllyn (2 miles)
Gauge   1ft 11½in
Open   Mar/Oct except Sats; daily Jul/Aug.

This line runs along the north shore of Llyn Padarn, using the trackbed of an old slate railway between Dinorwic quarries and the sea near Caernarfon. Slate traffic ended in 1961 and eight years later work began on the present line. It opened in 1972, and now frequent trains, hauled by tank engines which once worked in the quarries, run along the lakeside. The slate history of the area is well displayed in the museum near Gilfach Dhu station, but allow plenty of time to see it!

Market Bosworth Light Railway (Battlfield Line)

Shackerstone Station, Shackerstone,
Nr Market Bosworth, Leics.
Tel. 01827 880754(w/e), 01530 271721(Mon/Fri eves)
Route   Shackerstone-Shenton (4.75 miles)
Gauge   Standard
Open   Sun, Bank hols Easter/end Oct;
         sta mus op 11.30-5.30 w/e; events.

Shackerstone was the junction for a line to Loughborough, but passenger services ceased in 1931. After taking over a derelict station in 1970 it was nine years before the Society began running trains to Market Bosworth. Shenton, close to Bosworth battlefield was always the target, attained on 2nd August 1992. The former station is now a visitor centre. Small tank engines and ex-BR carriages form the trains, using an attractive route beside the Ashby canal.

Middleton Railway

Moor Road, Hunslet, Leeds, LS10 2SQ.
Tel. 0113 271 0320
Route   Moor Road-Middleton Park (1.25 miles)
Gauge   Standard
Open   Please telephone for details.

The oldest railway with an Act of Parliament (1758), the first to use steam commercially and the first standard gauge line to be run by a preservation society, which began operations on 18th June 1960. Freight was carried at first, but since this ceased the Middleton has been a passenger enterprise. Projects outstanding are a museum at Moor Road and an extension to Middleton Park at the southern end. The locomotives are all small, including some unique examples; carriages are converted Southern Railway luggage vans.

Ex-LNER 0-4-0VB Sentinel locomotive No.54 as restored on the Middleton Railway, August 1989.

Midland Railway Centre

Butterley Station, Ripley, Derbyshire, DE5 3TL.
Tel. 01773 570140
Route   Hammersmith-Ironville (3.5 miles)
Gauge   Standard - also 2ft and 3½in running
         lines
Open   Suns; Sat Apr/Oct, Dec; daily Easter &
         Spr BH wks; Tues/Sun sch summer hols.

The idea for this project dates from 1969, when a collection of Midland Railway-connected items was begun. Work started at Butterley in 1973, the first passenger train leaving there eight years later. Since then the line has expanded in both directions, opened a narrow gauge line (1991) and has gained a reputation for quality restoration work. The culmination of this was the museum at Swanwick Junction, opened on 19th June 1990: projects still to come are an extension to a terminus at Pye Bridge.

Nene Valley Railway

Wansford Station, Stibbington,
Peterborough, PE8 6LR.
Tel. 01780 782854/782921(tt)
Route   Yarwell Junction-Peterborough
         (7.5 miles)
Gauge   Standard
Open   w/e Apr/Oct plus midweek Jul/Aug;
         Suns only Nov; Special events.

Operations by the Peterborough Railway Society began in the late 1960s. Since 1974 Wansford has been their headquarters and has become the leading centre for foreign locomotives in the UK. On 30th June 1986 an extension to a new station at Peterborough Riverside was opened, and a site there is earmarked for Railworld, an international railway museum. Locomotives are large, mostly, and there is a mix of ex-BR and overseas carriage stock for passengers to travel in.

Northampton & Lamport Railway

Pitsford & Brampton Station, Chapel Brampton, Northampton.
Tel. 01604 820327
Route   On station site (0.75 mile)
Gauge   Standard
Open   Sundays.

Traffic on the Northampton to Market Harborough line ceased on 16th August 1981 and a group was formed to take it over. After a while things began to move, but it is only in the last few years that progress on the ground has been visible. A Polish tank engine arrived in 1992, and an appeal was launched to save more of the same. By the following year the intention was to re-open Lamport Crossing, but no passenger trains had run at that time.

Northants Ironstone Railway Trust

Hunsbury Hill Industrial Museum & Railway,
Hunsbury Hill Road, Camp Hill, Hunsbury,
Northampton, NN6 0PH.
Tel. 01604 890229
Route   Within site (2.25 miles)
Gauge   Standard
Open   10.00am-5.00pm most days, including
         weekdays, bank hols.

The project from the outset has been to restore part of the Hunsbury Hill Ironstone Railway, and it began with the acquisition of a station building in 1975. Passenger services began in May 1982. By 1988 two miles of track was in use, and the group owned four steam engines and six diesels. A museum includes documents, photographs and other artefacts relevant to the Northamptonshire ironstone industry.

North Yorkshire Moors Railway

Pickering Station, Pickering, North Yorkshire.
Tel. 01751 472508/473535(tt)
Route   Grosmont-Pickering (18 miles)
Gauge   Standard
Open   Telephone for details

This railway uses one of the country's earliest lines, engineered by George Stephenson and opened in 1836, for its route. BR closed it in 1965, and two years later a preservation scheme began. It was six years before the first train ran on what is now the second-longest preserved line in the country. A repair shop has been established at Grosmont, and big engines haul passengers in ex-BR stock through Newtondale Gorge to Pickering. The line is often visited by privately-owned locomotives.

Paignton & Dartmouth Steam Railway

Queens Park Station, Torbay Road, Paignton,
South Devon, TQ4 6AF.
Tel. 01803 555872
Route   Paignton-Kingswear (7 miles)
Gauge   Standard
Open   Easter, BH, Sun, Tues, Thur Apr, early
         May, Oct; daily end May/end Sept;
         special events.

This was once a broad gauge railway, but became standard in 1892. BR closed the line in 1971: the Dart Valley Railway Company bought it and began services on New Year's Day 1973, and also worked the Buckfastleigh line (qv South Devon Railway) until 1991. The Kingswear branch is operated as a GWR branch with (mostly) ex-GW locomotives and chocolate and cream liveried ex-BR carriages. Among these is an observation car which, between 1947 and 1951, ran on the Devon Belle express.

Peak Rail

Darley Dale, Matlock, Derbyshire.
Tel. 01629 580381/733476(w/e)
Route   Darley Dale-Matlock (2 miles)
Gauge   Standard
Open   Telephone for details.

The Midland Railway's line from Matlock to Buxton closed in 1968. It was 1975 before a society took over the trackbed and an uphill struggle. Developments were made at Buxton and progress elsewhere, but other than short runs in Buxton yard it was not until December 1991 that the first trains ran. There is still much to do before the group's objective of opening between Matlock and Buxton is achieved. At present it is a 'small engine' operation with ex-BR coaches, but, make no mistake, it will be a spectacular run when it is all open.

Plym Valley Railway

Marsh Mills Station, Coypool Road, Marsh Mills,
Plymouth, PL7 4NL.
Route   Marsh Mills-Plym Bridge (1.25 miles
         under construction)
Gauge   Standard
Open   Site daily, dawn to dusk; shop and cafe
         w/e only.

This scheme is perhaps best described as an embryo project at present: it aims to re-open the branch from Marsh Mills to Yelverton, once the London & South Western Railway's route to Plymouth but closed by BR in 1962. It was 1980 before a group settled on this site: much stock collection and track clearance has gone on since, but there have been many setbacks, now seemingly overcome. Steam locomotives and ex-BR stock will be the order of the day, but services are limited at present.

Pontypool & Blaenavon Railway

Nr Big Pit, Blaenavon, Gwent.
Tel. 01495 772726 (7pm-9pm only)
(Correspondence to: Council Offices, Lion Lane,
Blaenavon, Gwent, NP4 9QA)
Route   Within site (0.75 mile)
Gauge   Standard
Open   Telephone for details.

The original plan was to re-open the entire eight miles of the old London & North Western line between

Pontypool and Blaenavon, closed by BR in 1980. First activity centred around the historic Big Pit Mining Museum, and services began at Easter 1985. After successful operation of two miles of track the Society is now faced with finding a new site. Operations have contracted temporarily, pending further developments.

Ravenglass & Eskdale Railway

Ravenglass Station, Ravenglass,
Cumbria, CA18 1SW
Tel. 01229 717171
Route   Ravenglass-Eskdale (Boot) (7 miles)
Gauge   15in
Open   daily Apr/1st Nov, 26th Dec/1st Jan;
         some w/e Nov, Feb.

There has been a railway along Eskdale for well over 100 years, though it was at first at 3ft gauge rather than 15in. It served haematite (iron ore) mines, but after these closed the gauge was converted in 1927. Then came hard times: only purchase at auction in 1962 saved it, and it has now been turned into a thriving tourist attraction. Not only that, but the workshops at Ravenglass have built two steam engines for export to Japan, and the railway pioneered the use in the UK of radio control on trains.

Romney, Hythe & Dymchurch Railway

New Romney Station, New Romney,
Kent, TN28 8PL
Tel. 01679 362353/363256
Route   Hythe-Dungeness (13.5 miles)
Gauge   ·15in
Open   Daily end Mar/end Sept; w/e Mar, Oct.

Two racing drivers had the idea for this line, and though one was killed in 1924, the line opened three years later. In 1971 it was on the brink of closure, but it has battled on and survives. The locomotives are mostly one-sixth scale models of LNER 'Pacifics', but there are also two American outline engines and some diesels. Though the line has no spectacular scenery, the Kent marshes have their own special charm. Many of the area's schoolchildren depend on the railway to get them to their classrooms.

Severn Valley Railway

The Railway Station, Bewdley, Worcs, DY12 1BG.
Tel. 01299 403816/401001(tt)
Route   Bridgnorth-Kidderminster (16 miles)
Gauge   Standard
Open   daily March-November; Santa Specials
         December; Other spec events.

One of the market leaders in steam railways, the SVR was the trackbed of a line between Worcester and Shrewsbury. BR closed this in 1970, and four years later it was re-opened as a steam railway. The Society has an enormous collection of engines and stock, and the line has become a thriving enterprise. The quality of restoration work is high, and many private owners send their engines to Bridgnorth for overhaul. Many famous locomotives have visited, either for repair or for one of the regular galas.

Ex-GWR Manor class 4-6-0 No.7819 Hinton Manor *runs into Bewdley station, Severn Valley Railway, 3rd September 1991.*

Sittingbourne & Kemsley Railway

Milton Road, Sittingbourne, Kent.
Tel. 01634 852672/0795 424899(tt)
Route   Sittingbourne-Kemsley (1.5 miles)
Gauge   2ft 6in
Open   Contact Mr.M Burton, 85 Balmoral Road,
         Gillingham, Kent, ME7 4QG.

The first part of this line opened in 1906 to carry paper to the mill from a wharf on Milton Creek, and kept the mill in production throughout the Great War. A second mill was built at Kemsley, and when road transport took over, the paper company arranged for the survival of the line. An operating Company was formed by the Locomotive Club of

Great Britain, and now works the line using engines originally built for it. Passengers enjoy views of the marshes from carriages built for the nearby Chattenden & Upnor Railway.

Snowdon Mountain Railway

Llanberis, Caernarfon, Gwynedd, LL55 4TY.
Tel. 01286 870223
Route   Llanberis-Snowdon Summit (4.75 miles)
Gauge   2ft 7⅝in
Open   daily mid-March/beginning
         November.

This line is unique in Great Britain for two reasons - its gauge and its rack and pinion traction. It opened in 1898, closed the same day after an accident, and re-opened the following April. The line was entirely steam-worked until 1986, when diesels were introduced as an economy, and though more have now come the steamers still do much of the work. Each locomotive pushes a single carriage up to the summit, more than 100,000 passengers making this spectacular journey each year. Radio-control now copes with up to 48 train movements a day.

South Tynedale Railway

Alston Railway Station, Alston, Cumbria, CA9 3JB
Tel. 01434 381696
Route   Alston-Gilderdale (1.5 miles)
Gauge   2ft
Open   Easter-Oct, but with variations. Steam
         w/e, bank hols only.

In 1976 BR closed its branch between Haltwhistle and Alston, and preservationists planned to take it over as a standard gauge scheme. This was modified to the present gauge, and the first narrow gauge train ran in 1983. All but one of the steam locomotives is foreign, and the carriages, built new in 1991, have a continental air too. Gilderdale, the present northern terminus was reached in 1986: extension to Kirkhaugh is planned, then Slaggyford (5 miles), but this last is a long-term project.

Steamtown Railway Centre

Warton Road, Carnforth, Lancs, LA5 9HX.
Tel. 01524 732100
Route   within site (1 mile approx, each line)
Gauge   Standard, 15in
Open   Daily 9am-5pm Easter-Oct, 10am-4pm
         Nov-Apr. Special events.

Ex-LMS Pacifics Nos.6200 The Princess Royal *and* 46203 Princess Margaret Rose, *at Steamtown, Carnforth on 14th July 1991.*

Carnforth has had some ups and downs since the site became established as a steam centre after BR left it in 1967. Known mainly as a 'big engine' centre, some visitors are surprised to find a 15in gauge presence too, on the west of the site. The standard gauge line running to Crag Bank borders the opposite side, with shed, coaling tower and turntable near the 'starting' end. Many famous engines prepare for railtour duty here, and it is hoped that this will continue.

Strathspey Railway

Aviemore Speyside Station, Dalfaber Road, Aviemore, PH22 1PY.
Tel. 01479 810725
Route   Aviemore-Boat of Garten (5 miles)
Gauge   Standard
Open   Wed, Sat in Apr, Wed, Sat, Sun May & Oct, daily end May-end Oct

The trackbed used by this line was opened in 1863 as the main line between Perth and Inverness, and closed in 1965. Relaying began in 1972 and regular train services in 1979. Most of the buildings date from the 1860s. Large and small engines work here, and pride of the fleet is ex-Caledonian Railway 0-6-0 No. 828, returned to steam in 1993 after a long period as a static exhibit in Glasgow Transport Museum. An extension north to Grantown-on-Spey is planned.

Swanage Railway

Railway Station, Swanage, Dorset, BH19 1HB
Tel. 01929 425800/424276(tt)
Route   Swanage-Harman's Cross (3 miles)
Gauge   Standard
Open   Weekends; daily Christmas, Easter, Bank hols, peak running season

Using a branch line opened only in 1885 and closed in 1972, this Society has had problems in retaining its trackbed, which was almost used for a bypass. Visitors' facilities were available at Swanage by 1979, and slowly the line has been extended; to Herston (June 1982) and the present terminus in 1989. Corfe, the next goal, is almost in sight, but the final aim of Wareham is still some way off. Locomotives of all sizes can be seen here, and visiting engines come also.

Swansea Vale Railway

Llansamlet, Swansea
Tel. 01222 613299
Route   Within site (0.66 mile)
Gauge   Standard
Open   Telephone for details

This group, formed as the Lower Swansea Valley RPS in 1980, aimed to preserve the line between Swansea and Brynamman. Work began in 1984, and the first open day was held in August the following year. In 1986 the Group changed its name to the Swansea Vale Railway, but progress has been slow. A workshop was opened at Upper Bank, the ultimate destination.

Swindon & Cricklade Railway

Blunsdon Station, Tadpole Lane, Nr Swindon, Wilts.
Tel. 01793 771615(w/e)
Route   Within the Blunsdon site (0.5 mile)
Gauge   Standard
Open   W/e (telephone to check train operation)

Blunsdon station closed in 1937, though the line itself survived until the 1960s. A group took over the station area in 1979, and four years later were giving rides. A shed was in place by 1990, and with the recent reinstatement of a bridge south of Blunsdon, there is promise of going further. Though there are big engines at the site, the passenger work on such a short line is done by the small ones and visitors travel in ex-BR stock.

Talyllyn Railway

Wharf Station, Tywyn, Gwynedd, LL36 9EY.
Tel. 01654 710472
Route   Tywyn-Nant Gwernol (7.25 miles)
Gauge   2ft 3in
Open   Daily Easter-beg Nov, and over Christmas, New Year.

The first Preservation Society in the world took over this line in 1950, starting with the advantage that it was, at least, all there. The disadvantage was its very poor state. The first train under the Society ran in 1951, and the next year passengers reached Abergynolwyn. An extension along a disused mineral branch to Nant Gwernol opened in 1976, and in 1991 a new engine, largely built on site, went into service. This is one of the only lines where both original locomotives and stock (delivered in 1865/6) are still in regular service.

Tanfield Railway

Old Marley Hill, A6076 Road, Gateshead, Co.Durham.
Tel. 0191 274 2002
Route   Sunniside-East Tanfield (3 miles)
Gauge   Standard
Open   Daily. Trains on Sun & B/h, + Thur & Sat Jun, Jul, Aug. Spec events

This line dates from the earliest days of our railway history, having opened in 1725. BR closed it in 1968, the first private steamings happened two years later, and by 1977 the first stage of the line was open. Progress has been steady - Sunniside was reached in 1981 and East Tanfield a year later. Now members are heading for Burnopfield. No ex-BR coaches here - vintage ones, all superbly restored on the spot, are much more in keeping with the small engines that work the services.

Teifi Valley Railway

Station Yard, Henllan, Llandyssul, Dyfed, SA44 5HX.
Tel. 01559 371077
Route   Henllan-Pontprenshitw (1.5 miles)
Gauge   2ft
Open   Daily Easter/mid-October.

BR's goods traffic finally left this line in 1977, but it was a while before the preservation society became established. A mile of trackbed was cleared by 1985, and first trains ran in August that year, along three-quarters of a mile. The length of the line almost doubled with the opening, in 1990, of an extension to Pontprenshitw. The aim is to make a 6-mile line between Newcastle Emlyn and Llandyssul. The engines come from quarry lines in North Wales, and the carriages have been purpose-built.

Telford Steam Railway

The Old Loco Shed, Horsehay, Telford, Shropshire.
Tel. 01952 503880
Route   Within site
Gauge   Standard, 2ft
Open   W/e - telephone for details

The Telford Horsehay Steam Trust was founded in 1976 to restore locomotives and stock with a local connection. These would run on the Horsehay to Lightmoor branch, but, until then, open days would be held at the shed. Services along half a mile of track began in May 1984, and in 1990 the concern became the Telford Steam Railway. A 400-yard length of 2-foot gauge tramway was opened in 1991 so that members could use their steam tram, and an extra mile of trackbed was leased for the main line.

Tralee & Blennerville Steam Railway

Tralee, Co.Kerry, Republic of Ireland.
Tel. (010353) 066 28888
Route   Tralee-Blennerville (1.5 miles)
Gauge   3ft
Open   Daily April/September.

A very new line, this, funded by local authorities and the European Community, and opening on 20th July 1992. It runs along the trackbed of the old Tralee & Dingle Light Railway, and uses one of the original engines, recently repatriated after 25 years in America. The carriages come from Spain, and there is a well-equipped workshop at Blennerville.

Welsh Highland Railway

Porthmadog, Gwynedd, LL49 9DY.
Tel.   In season: 01766 513402/ Out of season:
         0151 608 1950(day)/0151 327 3576(eve)
Route   Portmadoc–Pen-y-Mount (0.75 mile)
Gauge   1ft 11½in
Open   Easter/end Oct.

The original Welsh Highland Railway had a very chequered career, and finally closed in 1937 having run at a loss for years. A 'revival' group began in 1964, bought the site of an old slate siding at Porthmadog BR station in 1976, and in 1980 began running trains. There are now four steam engines, one of which worked on the line originally, and carriages have been built at the Gelerts Farm workshop. It is hoped to extend the line north eventually, towards the mountains and Aberglaslyn.

Welshpool & Llanfair Light Railway

The Station, Llanfair Caereinion, Powys, SY21 0SF.
Tel. 01938 810441
Route   Welshpool-Llanfair Caereinion (8 miles)
Gauge   2ft 6in
Open   Daily Easter b/h, mid-Jul/early Sep;
         Tues/Thur mid-Jun/mid-Jul.

Opened in 1903, this was one of the first railways built under the 1896 Light Railways Act, and it has some of the steepest gradients found on adhesion railways in Britain. The line was worked by the Cambrian Railways, the GWR (which closed it to passengers in 1931) and then BR, which closed it completely in 1956. A Preservation Society took over and re-opened the first section to passengers in 1963. A new terminus in Welshpool came in 1982, and now a mixture of original and foreign rolling stock carries the visitors.

West Lancashire Light Railway

Station Road, Hesketh Bank, Nr Preston, Lancs, PR4 6SP.
Tel. 01772 815881
Route   Delph-Becconsall (430 yards)
Gauge   2ft
Open   Suns Apr/Oct plus b/h Suns, Mons;
         special events.

A scheme around two sides of an old claypit was begun by six schoolboys in 1967. This was a false start, but tracklaying on the present site began that year, and stock began to arrive. The first steam engine, *Irish Mail*, arrived in 1969 as a kit of parts, and another came in 1972. This was later sold to the Bala Lake Railway, but steam trains began running in 1980. The line celebrated its Silver Jubilee in 1992, and future plans include a 200-yard extension beyond Delph.

West Somerset Railway

The Railway Station, Minehead, Somerset, TA24 5BG.
Tel. 01643 704996/707650(tt)
Route   Minehead-Bishops Lydeard (20 miles)
Gauge   Standard
Open   Daily Good Fri/Oct, except some Mon
         & Fri in Apr, May, Sep, Oct.

The longest preserved railway in the country, in any gauge, is based on a broad gauge branch line opened in 1862. Converted to standard gauge 20 years later, BR closed it in 1971. The first 'preserved' train ran in 1975 but difficult financial years followed. The storms were weathered, however, and now trains of ex-BR carriages, and using all sorts of motive power, traverse the line. The quality of restoration to stations and other buildings is splendid, and the Somerset & Dorset Joint Railway Trust has an interesting centre at Washford.

Left *Ex-S&DJR 2-8-0 No.53808 runs round at Bishops Lydeard on the West Somerset Railway, July 1991.*

MUSEUMS AND OTHER CENTRES

Alderney Railway

PO Box 75, Alderney, Channel Islands.
Tel. 01481 823260
Route   Braye Road - Mamez Quarry (2 miles)
Gauge   Standard.
Open   Easter Eve-last Sun in Sept, pm w/e &
         b/h. Extra servs 1st wk Aug.

The Alderney Railway Society was formed in 1978.
The first steam services ran at Easter 1982, and now
visitors travel in ex-London Transport tube coaches.

Alford Valley Railway

Haughton House, Alford, Grampian.
Tel. 0197 55 2326
Route   Within Park (3.25 miles)
Gauge   2ft
Open   11am-5pm daily June, Jul, Aug; w/e only
         Apr, May, Sept.

Work began early in 1979, and the first section
opened that June. Services are steam or diesel, and
the scheme is complementary to the Grampian
Region Museum of Transport.

Amberley Chalk Pits Museum

Houghton Bridge, Amberley, Arundel, W Sussex,
BN18 9LT.
Tel. 01798 831370
Route   Amberley-Brockham, & industrial ext
         (500yd passenger, 300yd demo)
Gauge   2ft, also 100yd of 3ft 2½in
Open   Wed-Sun each wk & b/h; daily in school
         summer hols.

A museum of the industrial history of southern
England, sited in a worked-out chalkpit. There is a
large collection of steam and diesel industrial
locomotives, and a wide range of stock.

Audley End Miniature Railway

Audley End, Saffron Walden, Essex, CB11 4JG
Tel. 01799 541354
(Enq to: Estate Office, Buncketts, Wendon's Ambo,
Saffron Walden, Essex, CB11 4JL).

American outline No.24, Linda, *sets out on a circuit
of the Audley End Railway in April 1993.*

Route   Return loop within estate (1.25 miles)
Gauge   10¼in
Open   Daily Easter wk, summer h/term, sch
         hols; w/e, b/h mid-Mar-end Oct

Tracklaying began in 1963 and the first section was
opened the following year. The line reached its
present length in 1979, and now has three steam and
three diesel locomotives running in service.

Beamish Open Air Museum

Beamish, Co.Durham, DH9 0RG
Tel. 01207 231811
Gauge   Standard - static railway exhibits
Open   Daily Apr-Oct 10am-6pm; Nov-Mar (ex
         Mon) 10am-5pm.

An extensive site covering much more than railways,
though this is the home of the replica *Locomotion
No.1*. There is also a range of typical North Eastern
Railway buildings to the north of the site.

Birmingham Museum of Science & Industry

Newhall Street, Birmingham, B3 1RZ.
Tel. 0121 236 1022
Open   Throughout the year

The display covers much more than railways,
though there is a good collection of locomotives -
one main-line, several industrial - and other items
of railway interest.

Birmingham Railway Museum

670 Warwick Road, Tyseley, Birmingham, B11 2HL.
Tel. 0121 707 4696
Route   Within site (0.33 mile)
Gauge   Standard
Open   Daily 10am-4.30pm, w/e 10am-5pm.

A large collection of engines, based around the old
railway repair shop at Tyseley. Maintenance work
goes on here, and rides are available most weekends
and bank holidays.

Bressingham Railway Museum

Bressingham, Diss, Norfolk, IP22 2AB
Tel. 01379 88386/88382(tt)
Route   Four, all within the site.
Distances Standard & 9¼in both 0.25 mile,
           2ft & 15in both 2.25 miles.
Open   Daily Easter-Oct 10am-5.30pm; Steam
           Thur, Sun, b/h, & Wed in Jul, Aug

A large amount of railway interest here in its four
different lines, with static dispays of steam (rail and
road) engines too. Not to mention the funfair,
gardens and garden centre...

Bristol Harbour Railway

Bristol Industrial Museum, Princess Wharf, Bristol,
BS1 4RN.
Tel. 0117 925 1470
Route   Within Harbour limits (0.5 mile)
Gauge   Standard
Open   Apr-Oct.

The railway is an adjunct to the Bristol Industrial
Museum, which covers more than just railways.
Among much on view is Brunel's iron ship *Great
Britain*, now restored at the Great Western Dry Dock.

Cadeby Light Railway

The Old Rectory, Cadeby, Nuneaton, Warwicks,
CV13 0AS.
Tel. 01455 290462
Route   Within Rectory garden (approx 220
         yards)
Gauge   1ft 11½in and 5in
Open   Second Sat in every month, plus special
         events.

The Cadeby Light Railway had its first open day in 1963 and has given immense pleasure to thousands ever since. There is a large model railway, and the Rectory itself houses a collection of railwayana.

Caerphilly Railway Centre

Harold Wilson Estate, Van Road, Caerphilly, Mid-Glamorgan.
Tel. 01633 273182
Route   Within site (660 yards)
Gauge   Standard
Open   Every Sun pm, occasional steam days - telephone for details.

The Centre was founded in 1973 and Taff Vale Railway No.28 had been restored and steamed for TVR150 on 28th June 1986. Track is being extended towards the BR station.

Cambrian Railways Society

Oswald Road, Oswestry, Shropshire.
Tel. 01691 671749
(Enq: The Sec, Delamere, Old Church Road, Gobowen, Oswestry, Salop, SY11 3LH)
Route   Within Oswestry station limits (400 yards)
Gauge   Standard
Open   Daily 10am-4pm - running days enquire as above)

The railway items, collected in the station yard, share premises with the Oswestry Bicycle Museum. The oldest engine in an interesting collection is a 0-4-0ST built by Beyer-Peacock in 1879.

Chinnor & Princes Risborough Railway

c/o Peter Harris, 20 Daleford Road, Aylesbury, Bucks, HP21 9XD.
Tel. 01296 433795
Route   Chinnor-Princes Risborough (6 miles, under restoration)
Gauge   Standard
Open   Telephone for details.

One of the newer schemes - an open day was held at Chinnor cement works in 1991. Much must be done before the whole line can be open, but in the meantime steam can be seen at open days.

City of Liverpool Museum

William Brown Street, Liverpool, L3 0AA.
Tel. 0151 207 0001
Open   Telephone for details

A collection of vehicles of all sorts - in the railway section is the Liverpool & Manchester locomotive of 1838, *Lion*, though this, the oldest working locomotive in the world, is occasionally away on tour.

Conwy Valley Railway Museum

The Old Goods Yard, Betws-y-Coed, Gwynedd.
Tel. 01690 710568
Route   Within site (1.25 miles)
Gauge   7¼in
Open   Daily Easter-end Oct 10am-5.30pm

A small museum covering the whole railway scene, particularly in North Wales. A collection of standard gauge vehicles stands outside, and the miniature railway is passenger-carrying.

Corris Railway Museum

Corris Station Yard, Corris, Machynlleth, Powys, SY20 9SH.
Route   Corris-Maespoeth (0.75 mile, but not yet in public use)
Gauge   2ft 3in
Open   Museum only at present, write for details.

The museum, with several items from the Corris Railway's past, is housed in the old station building, while the line outside is being upgraded for passenger use.

Crewe Heritage Centre

see RAILWAY AGE

Darlington Railway Centre & Museum

North Road Station, Darlington, Co.Durham, DL3 6ST
Tel. 01325 460532
Route   Within museum limits (0.25 mile)
Gauge   Standard
Open   Daily 9.30am-5pm except during Christmas & New Year holidays.

A large collection of locomotives, models and artefacts, housed in the station that once served the first steam railway in the country. Steam weekends are occasionally held - telephone or write for details.

East Anglian Railway Museum

Chappel & Wakes Colne Station, Station Road, Wakes Colne, Essex, CO6 2DS.
Tel. 01206 242524
Route   Within station limits (0.33 mile)
Gauge   Standard
Open   Daily 9.30am-5pm; steam 1st Sun in month Mar-Oct, b/h, Wed in Aug.

A long-established scheme based around the Great Eastern Railway goods shed at Chappel. A large collection of freight vehicles can be seen, and several Victorian passenger coaches.

East Kent Light Railway

Shepherdswell Station, Nr Dover, Kent.
Tel. 01233 645576/01304 822850
Route   Within site
Gauges   Standard and miniature
Open   Ring for details

This scheme has been some time in taking off, but a Light Railway Order was signed in 1993 and BR agreed to sell the trackbed. Limited services began in 1994.

Exmoor Steam Centre

Cape of Good Hope Farm, Bratton Fleming, North Devon.
Tel. 01598 710711
Route   Within the farm site (1 mile)
Gauge   12¼in
Open   Daily Apr-Oct, Sun throughout the year.

This line, laid in 1990, runs on a steeply-graded route giving fine views over Exmoor. Steam engines (3) and carriages are custom-built in the railway's workshop, and a fourth engine is on its way.

Fairbourne & Barmouth Steam Railway

Beach Road, Fairbourne, Gwynedd,
North Wales, LL38 2PZ.
Tel. 01341 250362
Route   Fairbourne-Barmouth Ferry (2.75 miles)
Gauge   12¼in
Open   Telephone for details

Until 1983 this was a 15in gauge line, but has since undergone something of a transformation. New locomotives and rolling stock have been supplied, and the line has been generally refurbished.

Sherpa, based on a Darjeeling Railway locomotive design, and seen at the Fairbourne & Barmouth Steam Railway on 4th September 1993.

Gloddfa Ganol - Narrow Gauge Railway Centre

Gloddfa Ganol Mountain Tourist Centre, Blaenau Ffestiniog, Gwynedd.
Tel. 0176 689 500
Open   Easter-Oct 10am-5.30pm

Over seventy narrow gauge steam/diesel engines make this the world's biggest such collection. This is sited in the world's largest slate mine, which gives an added interest to a visit.

Great Western Railway Museum

Faringdon Road, Swindon, Wilts.
Tel. 01793 493189
Open   Weekdays 10am-5pm, Sun 2pm-5pm;
        Closed Gd Fri, Chr Day, Box Day.

Great Western locomotives and artefacts are in a house built as a lodge for railway workers. It stands in a 'railway village' where a worker's house has been restored to its turn-of-the-century condition.

Hollycombe Woodland Railway

Hollycombe House, Nr Liphook, Hants.
Tel. 01428 724900
Route   Within grounds (0.5 mile)
Gauge   2ft and standard
Open   From Noon on Sun, b/h from Easter-
        Sept.

This small line gives a pleasant run within the grounds of Hollycombe House, on the way passing a quarry from which there are extensive views across the South Downs.

Irchester Narrow Gauge Railway Museum

Irchester Country Park, Irchester, Wellingborough, Northants.
Tel. 01604 844763/01234 750469
Gauge   1000mm
Open   Sundays

A collection of narrow gauge locomotives and stock associated with Northamptonshire and the East Midlands. Steam and demonstration weekends are held in the last full weekend of each month from March to October.

Kirklees Light Railway

Clayton West, Huddersfield, W Yorkshire, HD8 9PE.
Tel. 01484 865727
Route   Clayton West-Skelmanthorpe (2 miles)
Gauge   15in
Open   W/e all year, daily Easter-end Sep; op
        weekdays, Sat from 1pm, Sun & summer
        school hols from 11am.

This little line, built on the trackbed of an old Lancashire & Yorkshire branch, enjoyed its first full season in 1993. There are diesel and two steam locomotives.

Lappa Valley Railway

Lappa Valley Railway & Leisure Park,
St.Newlyn East, Newquay, Cornwall.
Route   Benny Mill-East Wheal Rose (1 mile)
Gauge   15in
Open   April-October

This pleasure railway offers a 2-mile return trip along the trackbed of the former Newquay to Chacewater branch line, closed by BR in February 1963.

Leadhills Light Railway

The Station, Leadhills, Lanarkshire.
Tel. A Smith, 0141 556 1061
Route   Leadhills towards Glengonnar (0.33 mile)
Gauge   2ft
Open   Services variable - telephone for details

Another newcomer, which like others, uses an old standard gauge trackbed. The first steam train (with a borrowed engine) ran in 1990, and regular steam weekends are now held.

London Transport Museum

Covent Garden, London, WC2E 7BB.
Tel. 0171 886 8557
Open   Daily 10am-6pm; closed 24, 25, 26th
        December.

The display here re-opened in December 1993 after refurbishment, and includes much of importance from London's railway history, both in locomotives and rolling stock.

Manchester Museum of Science & Industry

Liverpool Road Station, Castlefield, Manchester.
Tel. 0161 832 1830
Open   Daily 10am-5pm, except 24, 25, 26th
        December.

An important collection, sited in the oldest surviving passenger station in the country. Local science and industry is included, and there are train rides at weekends.

Mangapps Farm Railway Museum

Southminster Road, Burnham-on-Crouch, Essex, CM10 8QQ.
Tel. 01621 784898
Route   Within site (0.5 mile)
Gauge   Standard
Open   W/e 1pm-6pm, and Wed pm from Easter-Sep.

A quickly developing centre, which opened only in August 1989 and is now expanding. A variety of steam and diesel engines, with rolling stock, is on show.

Narrow Gauge Railway Centre
see GLODDFA GANOL

Narrow Gauge Railway Museum

Wharf Station, Tywyn, Gwynedd, LL36 9EY.
Tel. 01654 710472
Open   See TALYLLYN RAILWAY

A large collection of locomotives, wagons and artefacts from narrow gauge systems throughout the UK. Restoration and display of these continues.

National Railway Museum

Leeman Road, York, YO2 4XJ.
Tel. 01904 621261
Open   Weekdays 10am-6pm, Sun 11am-6pm; Closed 1st Jan, 24, 25, 26th Dec.

The justly-famous National Collection of Britain's railways, in two halls, the Great Hall having opened in 1992. Exhibits on display are frequently changed, and demonstration lines provide passenger rides.

North Downs Steam Railway

Stone Lodge Centre, Cotton Lane, Stone, Nr Dartford, Kent.
Tel. 01634 861879
Route   Within site (0.5 mile)
Gauge   Standard
Open   Sun, b/h; Sat from May-mid Sep incl

After a period at Chatham Dockyard, this group has now established a new centre near the south end of the Dartford crossing, where it is building a collection of locomotives and stock.

North Tyneside Steam Railway
see STEPHENSON RAILWAY MUSEUM

North Woolwich Old Station Museum

Pier Road, North Woolwich, London, E16 2JJ.
Tel. 0171 474 7244
Open   Mon-Wed, Sat 10am-5pm, Sun, b/h 2pm-5pm. Closed Thur, Fri.

In the excellently restored station building (and also on the platform beyond) the visitor will find a wide range of railway material, most of it with Great Eastern Railway or London connections.

Railway Age

Crewe Heritage Centre, Vernon Way, Crewe.
Tel. 01270 212130
Route   On site (300 yards of standard gauge, 0.75 mile of 7¼in gauge)
Open   Daily 10am-5pm, rides at w/e.

A growing collection of steam and diesel locomotives and rolling stock. Main line steam engines are occasionally stabled here between railtours, and give a changing and added interest.

Railway Preservation Society of Ireland

Whitehead Excursion Station, Castleview Road, Whitehead, Co.Antrim, N Ireland, BT38 9NA.
Tel. 01960 353567
Open   Easter Sun, Mon, Tues. Spec events, Santa trains on Dec Suns before 25th - contact above for details.

The RPSI 3-day Spring Railtour is justly famous, but limited vieweing of the Society's collection of stock is available at the above times. Groups are welcome, subject to advance warning in writing.

Rutland Railway Museum

Cottesmore Sidings, Ashwell Road, Cottesmore, Oakham, Rutland, LE15 7BX.
Tel. 01572 813203(site)/01780 62384(inf)
Route   On site (0.5 mile)
Gauge   Standard
Open   Telephone for details

The railway collection at Cottesmore concentrates on equipment from the local ironstone industry. There are steam and diesel locomotives, and a very comprehensive assembly of goods wagons.

Andrew Barclay 0-6-0ST Salmon *at the Rutland Railway Museum, Cottesmore, during June 1992.*

Scottish Industrial Railway Centre

Minnivey Colliery, Dalmellington, Ayrshire.
Tel. 01292 313579
Route   Within site (440yd)
Gauge   Standard
Open   Sat Jun-end Sep. Telephone for details of special events.

A steam centre and museum based around the Dalmellington Iron Company railway. Guided tours are available of a large collection of steam and diesel locomotives, and steam-hauled brakevan rides are available.

Southall Railway Centre

Southall, Middlesex, UB2 4PL.
Tel. 0181 574 1529 (R A Gorringe, eve, w/e only)
Open   Telephone for details

BR vacated this site in 1986, the Group moved in two years later and held its first open day in 1993.

Eight locomotives (6 steam) are kept here, with a variety of rolling stock, though facilities and limited at present.

Southport Railway Centre

Derby Road, Southport, Lancs, PR9 0TY.
Tel. 01704 530693
Route   Within site (600 yards)
Gauge   Standard
Open   Oct-Apr 1pm-5pm, Jun-mid Sep 1pm-4.30pm, Jul-Aug 10.30am-4.30pm.

A collection of locomotives, with a few items of rolling stock, kept in the old steam shed vacated by BR in 1966. Steam-hauled rides are available from June to mid-September.

South Yorkshire Railway

Barrow Road Railway Sidings, Barrow Road, Meadowhall, Wincobank, Sheffield, S9 1LA.
Tel. 01742 424405/451214
Route   Within site (0.75 mile)
Gauge   Standard
Open   Telephone for details

Volunteers have led a wandering existence, but now have their main terminus at Meadowhall, alongside the shopping centre. The first open day at Chapeltown was held at Easter 1984.

Stephenson Railway Museum

Middle Engine Lane, West Churton, North Shields, NE29 8DX.
Tel. 0191 262 2627
Open   Daily Easter-Oct, except Mon, Tues.

In buildings which began life as the Tyne/Wear Metro Test Centre are displayed locomotives and exhibitions illustrating the progress of railways from wagonways to the present time. The North Tyneside Steam Railway connects the Museum with Percy Main Metro station.

Swansea Industrial & Maritime Museum

Museum Square, Maritime Quarter, Swansea, SA1 1SN.
Tel. 01792 650351
Open   Tue-Sun 10.30am-5.30pm.
        Closed Mon, 1st Jan, 24, 25, 26th Dec.

Many relics from Swansea's industrial past are displayed here, including some railway material, which is housed on the former dock sidings next to the museum.

Timothy Hackworth Museum

Solo Street, Shildon, Co.Durham.
Tel. 01388 777999
Open   Telephone for details

Steam locomotives are here on static display in a museum devoted to Timothy Hackworth, one of the under-rated railway pioneers. Also on view are many of Hackworth's papers and personal belongings.

Ulster Folk & Transport Museum

Cultra, Holywood, Belfast, BT18 0EU.
Tel. 01232 428428
Open   Variable - telephone for details.

Railway exhibits here have a special gallery, the largest Transport Museum gallery in Ireland. Other parts of the 45-acre site cater for different transport interests.

Welsh Industrial & Maritime Museum

Bute Street, Cardiff.
Open   Tue-Sat, b/h 10am-5pm, Sun 2.30pm-5pm. Closed Mon(ex b/h), 1st Jan, Gd Fri, 24, 25, 26th Dec.

A large museum where the story of transport in Wales is told in a variety of exhibitions. There is a full-scale replica of Trevithick's Pen-y-Daren locomotive of 1804.

Wells & Walsingham Light Railway

Wells-next-the-Sea, Norfolk, NR23 1QB.
Tel. 01328 856506
Route   Wells-Walsingham (4 miles)
Gauge   10¼in
Open   Daily Good Fri-end Sept.

Using trackbed left by a standard gauge branch, this line, opened in 1982, gives a ride inland behind steam, perhaps using *Norfolk Hero*, the largest 10.25in gauge engine ever built.

GREAT WESTERN RAILWAY. •
— NOTICE —
ALL PERSONS ARE WARNED NOT TO
TRESPASS UPON THE RAILWAYS OR STATIONS OF
THE COMPANY AND NOTICE IS HEREBY GIVEN
THAT PURSUANT TO THE PROVISIONS OF THE
COMPANY'S ACTS EVERY PERSON WHO TRESPASSES
UPON ANY SUCH RAILWAY OR STATION IN SUCH
MANNER AS TO EXPOSE HIMSELF TO DANGER OR
RISK OF DANGER RENDERS HIMSELF LIABLE TO A
PENALTY OF FORTY SHILLINGS AND IN DEFAULT
OF PAYMENT TO ONE MONTH'S IMPRISONMENT
FOR EVERY SUCH OFFENCE
BY ORDER